Cambridge Elements

Elements in the Problems of God
edited by
Michael L. Peterson
Asbury Theological Seminary

DIVINE MOTIVATION AND HUMANITY

Jordan Wessling
Lindsey Wilson College

Ross Parker
Charleston Southern University

Shaftesbury Road, Cambridge CB2 8EA, United Kingdom

One Liberty Plaza, 20th Floor, New York, NY 10006, USA

477 Williamstown Road, Port Melbourne, VIC 3207, Australia

314–321, 3rd Floor, Plot 3, Splendor Forum, Jasola District Centre, New Delhi – 110025, India

103 Penang Road, #05-06/07, Visioncrest Commercial, Singapore 238467

Cambridge University Press is part of Cambridge University Press & Assessment, a department of the University of Cambridge.

We share the University's mission to contribute to society through the pursuit of education, learning and research at the highest international levels of excellence.

www.cambridge.org
Information on this title: www.cambridge.org/9781009669382
DOI: 10.1017/9781009287074

© Jordan Wessling and Ross Parker 2025

This publication is in copyright. Subject to statutory exception and to the provisions of relevant collective licensing agreements, no reproduction of any part may take place without the written permission of Cambridge University Press & Assessment.

When citing this work, please include a reference to the DOI 10.1017/9781009287074

First published 2025

A catalogue record for this publication is available from the British Library

ISBN 978-1-009-66938-2 Hardback
ISBN 978-1-009-28705-0 Paperback
ISSN 2754-8724 (online)
ISSN 2754-8716 (print)

Cambridge University Press & Assessment has no responsibility for the persistence or accuracy of URLs for external or third-party internet websites referred to in this publication and does not guarantee that any content on such websites is, or will remain, accurate or appropriate.

For EU product safety concerns, contact us at Calle de José Abascal, 56, 1°, 28003 Madrid, Spain, or email eugpsr@cambridge.org

Divine Motivation and Humanity

Elements in the Problems of God

DOI: 10.1017/9781009287074
First published online: May 2025

Jordan Wessling
Lindsey Wilson College

Ross Parker
Charleston Southern University

Author for correspondence: Jordan Wessling, wesslingj@lindsey.edu

Abstract: Theists maintain that God created the world and acts within it. However, opinions divide regarding the motives that rest behind and systematically structure God's actions *ad extra*, especially those actions pertaining to humanity. The major paradigms differ as to whether God is principally motivated (i) by the goal of glorifying Himself, or (ii) by the demands of His own holiness, or (iii) in perfect conformity to moral norms, or (iv) by perfect love. The challenge of providing a theoretical framework for understanding God's fundamental motives vis-à-vis creation constitutes the problem of divine motivation. This Element addresses this problem from a Christian perspective. It assesses leading divine motivational frameworks concerning God's engagement with humanity, and it defends one framework in particular: the Agapist Framework. According to this preferred framework, God's actions toward humans are fundamentally motivated by God's perfect love.

Keywords: divine motivation, divine holiness, divine love, divine glory, divine deliberation, why did God create?

© Jordan Wessling and Ross Parker 2025

ISBNs: 9781009669382 (HB), 9781009287050 (PB), 9781009287074 (OC)
ISSNs: 2754-8724 (online), 2754-8716 (print)

Contents

1 The Problem of Divine Motivation 1

2 The Glorificationist Framework 5

3 The Holiness Framework 19

4 The Morality Framework 34

5 The Agapist Framework 42

6 The Plausibility of the Agapist Framework 54

7 Conclusion 63

References 66

1 The Problem of Divine Motivation

Theists maintain that God is a maximally great being who created the world and acts within it. However, opinions divide regarding the motives that rest behind and systematically structure God's actions *ad extra* (i.e., those actions that terminate outside the divine being), especially those actions pertaining to humanity. The major paradigms differ as to whether God is principally motivated (i) by the goal of glorifying Himself, or (ii) by the demands of His own holiness, or (iii) in perfect conformity to moral norms, or (iv) by perfect love. Each paradigm comes with a host of conceptual issues related to how the relevant paradigm might be understood, and why one might affirm it. Moreover, none of these paradigms is merely of theoretical interest (see Murphy 2021, 79–84). Rather, each informs additional theological doctrines that are often central to a given religious tradition (e.g., why God became incarnate and saves) and also bears upon wider questions related to God's existence (e.g., whether there are good reasons for God to be hidden or allow the manifold evils in the world). The challenge of providing a theoretical framework for understanding God's fundamental motives vis-à-vis creation constitutes the *problem of divine motivation.*

This Element addresses this problem by providing an opinionated survey of various divine motivational frameworks pertaining to God's engagement with humanity. The volume is a *survey* in that it canvasses leading contemporary divine motivational frameworks and accompanying arguments and objections. But, given space limitations, the examination of multiple refined versions of these frameworks will be minimal and theories that mix existing frameworks in numerous ways will be given only marginal attention. The focus will rather be on existing and well-defined divine motivational frameworks. This survey is *opinionated* in that each framework is evaluated and a partial defense of one particular framework is offered. We refer to our preferred framework as the Agapist Framework. According to it, God's actions toward humans are fundamentally motivated by God's perfect love. Roughly, God is *fundamentally* motivated by some character trait or consideration of His regarding humans if it substantially informs His treatment of humans and is generally prioritized over other motives God might have concerning humans. This volume focuses on the problem of fundamental divine motivation from a Christian perspective. Yet we also hope this work will be a resource to other monotheistic traditions and those interested in assessments thereof.

In approaching the problem of divine motivation from a Christian perspective, this Element is a work of philosophical theology. It is *philosophical* in that it engages contemporary philosophical scholarship, especially analytic philosophy of religion, and utilizes many of the affiliated modes of analysis. It is *theological* in that much of the reasoning relies upon core Christian doctrines. However, this work is also largely nonsectarian in the sense that the assessments of divine motivational frameworks are placed under the canons of typical philosophical adjudication, and, secondarily, it engages with voices outside of the Christian tradition, and theism more generally, as appropriate.

To suppose that God is motivated to perform some act or set of actions is to suppose that God is internally inclined (or, if one prefers, has reason of some weight or another) to perform that act or collection of actions. The notion that God's actions are fundamentally directed and structured by some motivational state or attitude assumes that God is necessarily predisposed to act in certain ways and not in others. This is not to assume, upfront, that God has only one fundamental motive, or cluster of such motives, from which God can never deviate. Nor do we mean to preclude the idea that God could adopt and act from motives contingently. Rather, the claim is that God has a certain character that necessarily predisposes God to perform some actions and not others (see Murphy 2021, 82–84). The present study concerns divine motivational frameworks that compete to explain the motives that God necessarily has regarding humans, should God decide to create them.

Theoretical frameworks about God's necessary motives serve to explain and predict divine action. They aim to shed light on the range of actions that God would, might, or is likely to perform. Divine motivational frameworks, then, are far-reaching theories or hypotheses about how God would be inclined to act, particularly (for the purposes of this Element) with respect to humans.

Two types of evidential support are particularly relevant for adjudicating between wide-reaching theories of this kind (see Swinburne 2004, ch. 3; Rutledge and Wessling 2023).

First, there is a given theory's *prior probability*. This is the theory's probability given all tautological information contained within the theory and an assessment of how it compares to other theories before considering the particular data that the relevant theories are supposed to explain. A theory's prior probability is determined by relevant background knowledge, proposed explanatory scope, simplicity/parsimony, and (as argued in Poston 2020) the number of unexplained contingencies or mysterious limitations (see Swinburne 2004, 67–68). But, crucially, a theory's prior probability need not be equivalent to a priori considerations alone. Considerations derived from experience, testimony, and the like are also relevant so long as these considerations are independent of the relevant data to be explained.

One key for evaluating the prior probability of divine motivational frameworks is what divine perfection would lead us to expect about divine motivation. We may think about this from the perspective of perfect being theology – the idea that maximal perfection or greatness is central to elucidating the concept of God (see Morris 1987; Hill 2005; Nagasawa 2017). Yet because our evaluations proceed on the assumption of Christian theism, doctrines about the divine nature that are peculiar to Christianity, such as the Trinity, but are neutral concerning competing motivational frameworks also factor into our prior probability considerations.

Second, there is a framework's *explanatory power*. As Richard Swinburne notes (2004, 56), "A theory has explanatory power in so far as it entails or makes probable the occurrence of many diverse phenomena that are observed to occur, and the occurrence of which is not otherwise to be expected." One may think about explanatory power in terms of the comparative *expectedness* of some phenomenon. We might say, for instance, that a given theory, T_1, has greater explanatory power than some alternative theory, T_2, whenever some observed phenomenon would be *more* expected on T_1 than on T_2. T_1 would then have greater explanatory power than T_2 with respect to the relevant phenomenon.

Various phenomena factor into a comparative analysis of the explanatory power of competing divine motivational frameworks. In this Element, one central consideration will be Christian Scripture's creation, redemption, and consummation arc, although data from other biblical themes will also be examined sometimes. Testimony from key theologians and philosophers likewise factors into the assessment of a framework's explanatory power. Finally, a framework's ability to account for the evil in the world and the occurrence of divine hiddenness will also be considered, though we cannot give this data the attention deserved.

In what follows, we assess divine motivational frameworks by comparing their prior probability and explanatory power relative to each other. Although each framework discussed has much to be said on its behalf, our conclusion is that the Agapist Framework (a version of the more general Love Framework) performs better overall than its competitors concerning these two dimensions of evaluation. Note: when comparing divine motivation frameworks, one can judge (i) that a hypothesis is more probable than the other hypotheses under consideration, or (ii) that a hypothesis is more probable than not. In the first case, the probability of the most probable hypothesis can be below 0.5, whereas the second judgment is that the overall probability of the hypothesis in question is above 0.5. Our claim that the Agapist Framework is comparatively more probable is an instance of the first type of conclusion.

However, we stress that our case for the Agapist Framework will be brief, partial, and rely on contentious premises, given the constraints of this volume. Hence, our goal is neither to establish conclusively that the Agapist Framework is the most plausible existing divine motivational framework nor to refute its competitors decisively. Instead, the goal is to provide a broad treatment of the relevant influential frameworks and to advance the discussion on how an overall comparative analysis of these frameworks might proceed, especially as this pertains to the advancement of the Agapist Framework. To keep this Element accessible to the widest possible audience, our comparative analysis will be presented informally, rather than stated in the rigorous language of contemporary confirmation theory.

Before moving to this assessment, we should address objections to the rational evaluation of divine motivational frameworks. One might think that considerations engendered by skeptical theism are at odds with our project. Skeptical theism can be understood as the claim that the phenomena of evil and divine hiddenness provide little to no evidence against the existence of God since we are unjustified in making all-things-considered judgments about what God would do or permit in any given situation. This kind of skepticism might be thought to extend to reasoning about God's motivations: humans are simply not well positioned to know what God's motives are and what their weights might be within divine deliberative processes. Relatedly, some theologians and philosophers regard talk of God acting for various reasons as much too anthropomorphic (e.g., Davies 2006; 2011). Hence frameworks regarding God's motives cannot approximate the truth of the matter.

One response to skeptical theism is to reject it by arguing that the skepticism advanced (i) undermines other theological or value judgments that we seem warranted in making (e.g., Swinburne 1998, 25–29; Hasker 2010; Ekstrom 2021, ch. 4) or (ii) gives us strong reason to be agnostic about God's existence (Climenhaga Forthcoming). However, many deny that skeptical theism has these implications. Some maintain that skeptical theism has a fairly narrow aim, focused on select inductive inferences germane to arguments against the existence of God. Thus, the skepticism supported by skeptical theism does not apply to many other judgments of value and theology (see Hendricks 2023a, 43–48 and 67–70). Importantly, moreover, many skeptical theists deny that their skepticism extends to being entirely unable to reason about divine motivations (e.g., Bergmann 2009, 377). There may be limits to our grasp of the realm of value and modality, for instance, yet we can reason about God's big-picture motivations. Some go further and attempt to provide a model for predicting certain divine actions that is compatible with skeptical theism (Hendricks 2023a, ch. 8).

Against what some skeptical theists would permit, we assume that humans can, with due care, reason about God's general motivations (and what they predict) as they pertain to humans – even if a healthy dose of skepticism about the particular actions God might perform on specific occasions is sometimes warranted. Only when deemed necessary will we return briefly to issues related to skeptical theism.

In response to the anthropomorphism objection to reasoning about divine motivations, note that philosophers and theologians of various traditions and backgrounds throughout the centuries have reasoned about the motives and character of God. We find this impetus as far back as Abraham asking "Shall not the Judge of all the earth do what is just?" (Gen. 18:25). It also seems central to Anselm of Canterbury's famous argument *remoto Christo* (i.e., apart from Christ as revealed in Scripture) for God's incarnation and atonement and to a significant strand of the Christian tradition that has inquired into something resembling divine motivational frameworks by assuming that divine and human reasons for action share certain similarities (see Wessling 2020a, 28–33). We follow this strand of the Christian tradition.

Additionally, our project of philosophical theology does not require that we have an exhaustive grasp of divine motivation. The claim is more circumspect: we can think about the big-picture structure of divine motives and evaluate which divine motive (if any) concerning humans most fundamentally inclines God to act in corresponding ways. Such reasoning will not be limited to philosophical reflection in this volume. Rather, as indicated, Christian Scripture will be relied upon considerably, which provides much data regarding divine motivations.

One final statement about the project. Assuming that theism is true, God certainly is a tremendously mysterious being. Yet many theists cannot help but consider the motivations that God necessarily has since several significant theological judgments are grounded in assumptions about why God does what He does. Thus, while aiming to think rightly about God's motives might be an enterprise liable to fall into error, it's a challenge that some of us simply cannot ignore. We hope that the following reflections advance the discussion on divine motives for those who feel similarly.

2 The Glorificationist Framework

Some Christians maintain that God creates and acts within creation not ultimately for the creature but for Himself. On one particularly prominent version of such a view, God's actions are principally motivated by His own glory, that is, the expression or display of the beauty of His attributes *ad extra*. We call this *glorificationism*: the view that self-glorification constitutes God's fundamental motivation for creating and ordering the events of this world, all other divine purposes or aims regarding creation being motivationally subordinate to God's self-glorification. This perspective is often rightly associated with the Reformed Christian tradition, but can plausibly be found in Lutheranism, Thomism, and some early Christian sources as well (Bavinck 2004, 430–435). In this section, we scrutinize glorificationism. To keep the section manageable, we focus on arguably the most significant representative of this glorificationist tradition, Jonathan Edwards. In focusing on Edwards, however, we also explore relevant quadrants of the affiliated logical space so that our conclusions may generalize more broadly. We argue that glorificationism has considerable liabilities which substantially threaten the viability of the framework.

The Character of Glorificationism

Glorificationism takes different forms. What unites them is the idea that God's fundamental motivation for creating and governing the world is to express or display the divine attributes through creation – to express divine beauty or excellency outside of the divine nature. Glorificationists may disagree about which attribute or attributes constitute God's self-glorification and which means God utilizes to achieve this self-glorification within creation. Nevertheless, it is important that a certain understanding of glorificationism is ruled out upfront.

It is tempting to explicate glorificationism in a way that breaks down the distinction between God acting for Himself and God acting for the sake of creatures. One might say, for example, that God glorifies Himself by expressing His love *ad extra* and that loving His creatures itself *constitutes* the divine glory. Thus, God glorifies Himself precisely by acting for creatures' sake (e.g., Crisp Forthcoming, ch. 10; McCall 2008, 239). Alternatively, one might suggest that God has many motives for His actions within creation, one of which is self-glorification another of which is self-giving love, and no one motive takes priority over the other. Hence there is no irreconcilable division between glorificationism and God creating out of the motive of other-directed benevolence.

Although one could adhere to either of these ways of characterizing divine motivation, such renderings are not forms of glorificationism as we use the term. "Glorificationism" as we mean it springs from the conviction that God's actions toward creation are fundamentally about expressing or displaying Himself *ad extra*. Benefiting creatures is subordinate to God's self-glorifying purposes. For example, consider the claims of the glorificationist Louis Berkhof, speaking specifically about the predestination of the elect for salvation: "The purpose of [God's] eternal election is twofold: (1) *The proximate purpose is the salvation of the elect.* [. . .] (2) *The final aim is the glory of God.* Even the salvation of men is subordinate to this" (2017, 56). Edwards affirms something similar. He is clear that, strictly speaking, it's the *"emanation of [God's] own infinite fullness"* itself that *"excited him to create the world"* (1989, 435; cf. 438–439). The goodness of communicating that fullness to creatures is derived from the more fundamental expressive purpose (see, e.g., Crisp 2012, 146; Schultz 2020, 15–16; Rigney 2023, 99–100 cf. McClymond & McDermott 2011, 207–223). Thus, on glorificationism, God's ultimate reason for creating is *Himself*. That which God does in love for His creatures, or from some other motivation, is done in service to His self-glorification.

The Argument from Reason

Jonathan Edwards's essay *Concerning the End for which God Created the World* (hereafter *End of Creation*) is, to our minds, the most detailed and sophisticated defense of glorificationism. In it, Edwards presents a two-part argument for the view. One part draws from reason unaided by special revelation and the other from Scripture. Though Edwards does not use this terminology, one could say the goal of the first part is to assign a high prior probability to glorificationism (see Edwards 1989, 419 and 463; cf. Rigney 2023, 106), whereas the goal of the second part is to affirm that glorificationism has considerably high explanatory power with respect to Scripture.

We begin the assessment with Edwards's argument from reason. The interpretation of this argument is debated (compare McClymond & McDermott 2011, 207–223 with Schultz 2014a, 2014b; 2020, 255–283). However, the following constitutes a plausible reconstruction of a significant part of this argument, sufficient for present purposes.

(1) God is the sole maximally great being.
(2) If God is the sole maximally great being, then God must value Himself infinitely.
(3) If God must value Himself infinitely, then God's highest original end for creation must be to express His attributes via creation.
(4) If God's highest original end for creation must be to express His attributes via creation, then God's dominant motivation for creating and interacting with creation must be to express the divine attributes *ad extra*, which is God's highest consequential end for creation.

So,

(5) God's dominant motivation for creating and interacting with creation must be to express the divine attributes *ad extra*, which is God's highest consequential end for creation.

The conclusion of this argument constitutes a version of glorificationism.

Comment on each of these premises is in order. (1) says that God is the unrivaled greatest possible being. Edwards (e.g., 1989, 422) affirms such an exalted conception of God, albeit in different language. This premise seems straightforward in terms of reflection on the concept of God. So we need not explain it further.

Behind (2) rests what McClymond (1995) terms the *principle of proportionate regard*: one ought to value things to a degree proportionate to their intrinsic worth. By implication, then, humans should be valued above dogs and plants because humans enjoy greater intrinsic worth. Given this principle, Edwards (1989, 426) maintains that it is essential to God's perfection to value Himself infinitely. For God to value Himself infinitely means, for Edwards, something like that God values Himself to a qualitatively unsurpassable degree *or* that God values Himself limitlessly (more on this subsequently). The result of God's infinite self-regard is that God values Himself well above the degree to which God values any creature. This is not divine narcissism in Edwards's view (*pace* Jordan 2020, 89–90). It is simply a matter of God respecting the value of the way things are (Edwards 1989, 450–451).

Furthermore, if God must value Himself above all else, God must value the expression of His attributes made possible by creation more than He does creation itself or any facet thereof. This is the core idea expressed within (3). But (3) also rests upon distinctions that Edwards (1989, 406–418) makes between various types of ends. Whereas *ultimate ends* are ends that are pursued for their own sake, *subordinate ends* are those which are pursued as means to, or else as a particular way of instantiating, another end. A *highest end* (or *chief end*) is a version of an ultimate end. A highest end is that which is sought for its own sake *and* is the most valued end among an integrated set of ultimate ends. A man who embarks on a journey may have two ultimate ends in mind: to find a spouse and to look through a new telescope. In this case, we may suppose that the former is the highest end since it outranks the value of the latter end. The burden of *End of Creation* is to argue that God's glory is the highest end for creation. It must be the highest end for creation since the manifestation of the divine glory is objectively a more valuable end than any other relevant end that God might pursue (e.g., creaturely happiness). Thus, given the principle of proportionate regard, God will value this manifestation of divine glory more than any alternative end. More precisely, Edwards argues that what might be called the *highest original end* for the world, as found in (3), is the expression of divine glory.

Further distinctions must be introduced to understand a highest original end. An *original ultimate end* is an ultimate end that one values or desires apart from all conditions and circumstances. This is distinct from a *consequential ultimate end*, which is valued or desired within a given context or on a given condition in light of the original ultimate end. Edwards provides the example of someone who is inclined toward relationships as his original ultimate end and so seeks to build a family as his consequential ultimate end. It might help to understand the distinction between original and consequential ultimate ends as between what one values abstracted away from concrete circumstances and conditions (one's original ultimate end) and the particular end one might pursue to actualize this abstract form of valuing (one's consequential ultimate end). The *highest* original end is one's most highly prized or valued original ultimate end. Hence, (3) is basically the claim that because God rightly values Himself infinitely, God's highest original end for creation available to Him is to exercise His attributes via creation.

Why would God's infinite valuing of *Himself* dispose God to make the *exercise of His attributes* His highest original end for creation? Edwards's answer runs along the following lines (see Schultz 2014a, 93–94, 2014b, 313–315). If God values Himself and hence the attributes He possesses infinitely (and given divine simplicity, God and His attributes are not separate), then God must value the exercise of those attributes of His character that can be expressed in worthwhile ways. Since God greatly values His power, He would greatly value putting His power to work in the creation and formation of the cosmos. Similarly, since God greatly values His wisdom, He would value the designing of a creation by that wisdom, and so on. Moreover, since God rightly values Himself and His attributes far more than He does any creature or potential creature (given that He is considerably more valuable than any creature or collection thereof), and since any divine creation necessarily includes some expression of God or exercise of some divine attribute, the highest original end for creation must be God's expressing Himself through it.

To this Walter Schultz (2014a, 100) adds another consideration which is implicit in Edwards's argument. Edwards thinks it is part and parcel of morality that one affirms what one values in action. Paired with the principle of proportionate regard, the idea is that God must value things in proportion to their goodness and affirm what He values in action. In further support of Edwards's argument, one might deduce that because God's self-valuing is infinite, God must affirm His superlative self-valuing in all of His actions, including those involving creation.

(3) could be read as implying that God necessarily creates, since God has only one possible highest original end for creation. However, (3) might also be read as indicating that God necessarily has a particular reason to act in a particular way, though the choice to act upon this reason is contingent. There is some

disagreement about how best to interpret Edwards on this score (e.g., Crisp 2012, 57–76; Rigney 2023, 122–128). Some commentators maintain that Edwards thought that God's creation of the world is contingent, whereas others demur. Either interpretation of (3) is acceptable. But we suspect that the majority will find Edwards's argument from reason most plausible if (3) is interpreted in a manner that allows for divine freedom concerning the contingency of creation. We have stated (3) accordingly.

(4) is the application of God's supposed highest original end to a specific creative act. Since God's highest original end for creation can only be to express His attributes, God's highest consequential end for creation must be to instantiate this. Because of this consequential highest end, moreover, God's dominant motivation for choosing to make and guide creation must be the noted self-glorification. Edwards reasons that if creation's *end* must ultimately be about divine self-glorification, then God's most significant *motivation* for creating must be similarly directed. In making such claims, Edwards distinguishes between *motives* (what induces or moves action) and *ends* (that at which an action is aimed). Edwards's argument from reason concerns the chief or highest end for which God created the world, not God's motivation *per se*. However, Edwards maintains that God is most motivated to do what God sets as His highest end, since God sets as His highest end that which is worthy of corresponding motives (e.g., Edwards 1989, 421–423). So, while Edwards does not use our language of a dominant motive, he does plausibly work with a suitably equivalent idea.

But what does it mean for God to be *dominantly motivated* by self-glorification? Edwards supplies no such concept for us. Yet the following seems to resonate with the spirit of Edwards: God is dominantly motivated to glorify Himself through creation in that this motive is absolutely prioritized above (or always outweighs or is intrinsically more significant than) any other motive God might have or act upon concerning creation. This is stronger than a fundamental motive as described in Section 1, and it is how language related to dominant motives is used in the remainder of this section.

That stipulation aside, we can see that once (1)–(4) are affirmed, the glorificationist conclusion in (5) follows. What we have then is a proof for glorificationism, which Edwards believes is also confirmed by Scripture.

Evaluating the Argument from Reason

There are many claims embedded within the reconstructed argument from reason to which one might object. For example, some philosophers have affirmed theses that if true would appear to entail the falsity of the principle of proportionate regard (e.g., Adams 1972; Leftow 2017). If this principle is false, this could be taken to undercut (2) and/or (3), depending upon certain interpretative details. Similarly, some theologians deny that God loves Himself more than creatures (e.g., Torrance 1996, 244), which would seem to cut against (3). Still others might doubt, against (4), that just because God has a highest original end for creation, He must be dominantly motivated to adopt it as His highest consequential end with His creation-regarding acts (see Leftow 2019). We focus on other objections to (3) and (4).

Recall that (3) is built on the idea that God values Himself infinitely. If God so values Himself, perhaps this precludes God from setting any chief end for creation other than divine glory (see Schultz 2014a, 93–94).

To suppose that God values Himself infinitely may be understood in two relevant ways (for a fuller catalog of options, see Göcke and Tapp 2019). It could be understood *qualitatively* to mean that God values Himself maximally or to the utmost fitting and worthwhile degree (see Oppy 2014, 36). The trouble with this understanding of infinite valuing is that it does not clearly preclude God from rightly valuing Himself *and others* in a manner that allows God to set an alternative highest original end from that which is found in (3). It is not clear, for example, that making the flourishing of creatures His chief end for creation entails any kind of denial of maximal self-regard on the part of God (see Wessling 2020a, 87–88). Hence, the qualitative view of divine self-regard does not entail (3).

A second understanding of infinite self-valuing is the idea of *limitlessness* (see Clayton 1997, 99–102; Pannenberg, 1991, 397–401). On this understanding, God values Himself infinitely because there is no boundary to divine self-valuing. Hence, God does not value Himself *and* the creature for their own sakes. That would be to place a boundary on God's self-valuing, since then there would be a form of divine valuing that is not a form of self-valuing. Thus, on this understanding of infinite self-regard, God at most values creatures only as a way of valuing Himself (see Schultz 2014a, 93–94). This second understanding of infinite self-valuing does support (3): God's highest original end for creation must be the manifestation of self-value.

Nonetheless, this second view on God's infinite self-valuing comes with a cost. It entails that God is unable to love creatures. If Jones values Smith (and advances Smith's good and wants to be in a relationship with Smith) only as a way of loving or expressing himself, then Jones clearly does not love Smith since Jones's affection is insufficiently focused on Smith (see Adams 1999, 155). Similarly, if God values creatures (and promotes their good and relates to them) only as a way of loving or expressing Himself, God plausibly does not love creatures since His affection would be insufficiently focused upon them (see Zagzebski 2004, 216). And if God *necessarily* values creatures only as a way of valuing Himself, it seems *impossible* for God to love creatures. This results in ruling out on a priori grounds the possibility of divine love for humans. To be sure, leading Christian theologians of the past have affirmed something similar (e.g., Augustine, *De Doctrina Christiana*, Book 1, chs. 22–40), though they would be quick to add that God bears an attitude toward us that is analogous to what we characteristically mean by love. Nevertheless, many will find the conclusion that God cannot love us in a straightforward sense intellectually unsettling (e.g., Brümmer 1993, 109–126). Those who think this are unlikely to take this path to affirming (3).

But let that objection to (3) pass. Even still, (3) faces another nearby challenge. Let *rich benevolence* refer to the kind of benevolence in which one gives to another primarily for the other's sake. Many theologians have thought that the capacity for rich benevolence is an excellence that a perfect God should possess (e.g., Dodds 1986, 300–301; Weinandy 2000, 160–161). In keeping with this conviction, Jonathan Kvanvig (1993, 116) maintains that instantiating self-giving love is part of "being the highest good," which involves "being motivated fundamentally by the welfare of the one loved." Behind such thinking rests the idea that since God is absolutely perfect, God must be able to exemplify the most valuable and fitting kind of love, including rich benevolence. The trouble is that such convictions about divine love are plausibly thought to be incompatible with (3) (and probably (4)), at least when the creature is in view.

The reason for this is straightforward (see Wessling 2020a, 97–99). Given glorificationism, every action that God performs concerning creation is primarily a self-focused action, if not directly then indirectly. Hence, God never acts primarily for the sake of His creatures. Furthermore, so long as it is held that glorificationism is the only framework for divine motivation that God might take up concerning creation, it follows that God necessarily cannot exemplify rich benevolence for any creature. Thus, glorificationism weakens the doctrine of divine benevolence substantially. There are significant ways in which God cannot exercise rich benevolence. If one finds this unacceptable, and if (3) leads to this conclusion, one has reason to reject (3).

The glorificationist might agree that God must be able to exemplify rich benevolence but deny God needs to have this capacity concerning creatures. Perhaps, instead, the persons of the Trinity necessarily exemplify rich benevolence for each other, thereby securing the full riches of divine love.

Be that as it may (and there are complications here to resolve), there remains a puzzle on glorificationism. Suppose God wants to glorify Himself by exercising graciousness and love toward creatures. Plausibly, if God wants to exemplify these features in their most valuable ways, God cannot be primarily motivated by self-glorification in His dealings with creatures. For God to love and exercise grace toward creatures in robustly valuable ways, such actions must be done primarily for them, for the reasons just considered. Indeed, as we have seen, to be gracious or loving toward others only insofar as one's more foundational self-glorifying purposes are advanced do not appear to be genuine expressions of love or grace. To that extent, a God who is interested in glorifying Himself via the expression of love and grace is best suited by *not* adopting self-glorification as His dominant (or even fundamental) motive for creation. Hence, a God who is motivated by the idea of glorifying Himself along the noted lines should, perhaps paradoxically, make such glorificationism a secondary motive for creation. In that case (4) would be false since (4) concerns the *motive* adopted in relation to God's highest consequential end for creation.

There are two lessons one might derive from this objection to (4). One might conclude that this objection reveals that glorificationism is incoherent. To make good on this claim, it would need to be shown that God's self-glorifying purposes through creation are best served by expressing love and grace toward creatures (perhaps because love, and by extension grace, reflects what is central to the intra-trinitarian life), and thus such divine self-expression would be essential to glorificationism. The unhappy result would be that if God is essentially motivated as the glorificationist supposes, then God would not be essentially motivated as the glorificationist supposes, since to be so motivated would entail that God cannot take up the goals needed to be so motivated. An alternative lesson might be that God has consequential ends and corresponding dominant motives for creation that are incommensurate in value. God could act for the reasons specified by glorificationism, however doing so means that God does not express His love and grace toward creatures in more valuable kinds of ways. Or God could act in accordance with another motivational framework, which may entail that certain goods related to divine self-glorification are lost. If one holds that God's ends and motives are incommensurate in this way, this calls into question (3). For (3) is built on the idea that a single highest original end for creation can be deduced from God's infinite self-regard. Yet no such deduction can be made if values are incommensurate in the described manner.

Consider one last attempt at defending (3) and secondarily (4) (Luke 2024). Suppose that God is The Good and that all creaturely goodness is derived from Him (e.g., Adams 1999). Based upon this axiological structure, someone might contend that any end that God seeks outside Himself is necessarily an end that resembles Himself. For God necessarily seeks that which is good, and there can be no good that is not Himself or derived from resembling Him. Being aware that He can only seek an end outside Himself that is good precisely in virtue of its resemblance to Him, it might further be thought that God necessarily seeks that which resembles His excellency, *because of this resemblance*, in His actions *ad extra*. So, God creates to instantiate or express some facet of His excellency as His highest affiliated end. In other words, God's creation-directed acts are necessarily directed toward self-glorification.

This defense of (3) and (4) requires a commitment to two theses. First, there is the axiological thesis that all goodness that is not God or a feature thereof is derived from God; such things are good in virtue of bearing a certain relation to God. Second, there is the motivational thesis that God's actions are necessarily directed at ends that resemble Himself *because they resemble Himself*. The present glorificationist defense of (3) and (4) relies upon the idea that the latter thesis follows from the former. We doubt this implication and the axiological thesis upon which it rests.

Consider the exemplarist doctrine of divine ideas as a credible alternative to the axiological thesis (see Kemp 2022). According to this alternative, God has ideas about Himself which act as something analogous to blueprints for creative possibilities. From these divine ideas the exemplarist maintains that God creates beings that exactly resemble or are qualitatively identical to some facet of God. Creatures are thereby copies of facets of the divine. On the assumption that every facet of God is intrinsically valuable and that evaluative properties supervene on (intrinsic or monadic) descriptive properties, it follows that every creature who exactly resembles some (descriptive) facet of God is intrinsically valuable (since the values supervene on the intrinsic descriptive features). On exemplarism, then, all creaturely values come from God, The Good, by being copies of facets of God and created by God to be so. Yet, contrary to the axiological thesis, the exemplarist denies that creaturely goodness is to be explained by a derivation relation to God's goodness.

Let us now ask why, given exemplarism, God loves Himself. Does God love Himself primarily because He is Himself, because this is the individual with whom He is most acquainted? Plausibly not. While such egoistic considerations might play some role in explaining God's self-love, a better answer seems to be that God loves Himself because He is beautiful, because He is valuable.

But now suppose, in keeping with exemplarism, that creatures have their own intrinsic value. If God loves Himself primarily because He is intrinsically valuable and creatures too enjoy intrinsic value, plausibly God loves creatures primarily because they are intrinsically valuable, not primarily because they are copies of Himself. But if God loves creatures for this reason, He probably acts for them similarly motivated by creaturely value. Insofar as this is so, exemplarism cuts against both the axiological and the motivational theses.

Suppose we grant the axiological thesis, however. Still, God plausibly loves Himself not primarily because He is Himself but because He is intrinsically valuable. Now, if creatures that derive their value are still somehow intrinsically valuable (see Rubio Forthcoming), then, plausibly, God loves creatures because they are intrinsically valuable and only secondarily because it is His value they reflect (see Wessling 2020a, 92–97). In other words, if God's love is primarily explained by the value of beings, and not by whether this value is His value or derived therefrom, God primarily loves creatures for whatever value they have, even if it is but a dim reflection of the value possessed by Him. But, as before, if God loves creatures for this reason, He probably acts for them similarly motivated by creaturely value, not primarily because they reflect Him. If this reasoning works, then we shouldn't hold that the motivational thesis follows from the axiological thesis.

However, lay that reasoning aside for the sake of argument. Suppose all creaturely value is derived from God and thus, in keeping with the motivational thesis, God's actions for creatures are necessarily dominantly motivated by the desire to express Himself via creatures. Given this, a now familiar problem emerges. If we agree that x cannot love another person y if all of x's actions toward y are predominantly motivated by x's desire for self-expression, it follows that God, as just characterized, cannot love creatures. We regard this as a reduction to the absurd.

But even overlooking that judgment, another problem arises. It seems right to say that one human, x, cannot love (or cannot love non-defectively) another human, y, if x exclusively, or predominantly, values y for the reason that y is an expression of goodness that x (rightly or not) prizes more (see Adams 1999, ch. 6). In such a case, the attitude that x bears to y is insufficiently focused on y to count as love for y, or at least a rich form of it. However, for one human to love another richly is incredibly valuable, limited in value though humans are. Yet, given the axiological thesis, this apparently rich love would be valuable only if it is derived from God in some way, probably because God loves creatures richly, limited in value though they are. But, given that God cannot love creatures richly on the motivational thesis, it seems that one human's love for another in the relevantly rich way cannot be valuable. So, we have an apparent contradiction between the pairing of the axiological and motivational theses and the conviction that it is valuable for one human to love another richly. It seems to us more plausible to cling to the latter conviction and reject the former wedding of theses.

One might appeal to intra-trinitarian love in response to this last objection. The value of a human's love for another is derived from the way the Father loves the Son, for example. Just as the Father loves the Son in a way that is sufficiently focused on the Son, the human may love another in way that is sufficiently focused on the beloved. The value of latter rich love is derived from the former love.

But this response fails. Our objection is that a human's rich love for another human is valuable despite the fact that humans are limited in value and perhaps derive their value from God. But this is not the case with intra-trinitarian love. The Son is not limited in value and He plausibly does not derive His value from another.[1] The Father's love of the Son is therefore not a case where it's valuable for one being to love another richly even though the beloved being possesses limited and derived value. Yet it is clearly valuable for one human to love another richly despite the limitations of human value. There seems to be no way of grounding the value of this human-to-human love on the conjoining of the axiological thesis with the motivational thesis. We find it more plausible to affirm the value of rich human-to-human love than we do the coupling of these theses. Those who judge similarly have reason to reject the defense of glorificationism that relies on these theses.

A good argument is one in which an individual is justified in believing the conclusion based on its premises. The reconstructed argument from reason for glorificationism does not obviously clear that threshold, even with the help of the auxiliary principles discussed. But perhaps the considerations embedded within this argument from reason can be utilized in favor of a probabilistic argument on behalf of glorificationism. The basic idea would be that the prior probability that God's creation-regarding acts would be dominantly (or fundamentally) motivated by self-glorification is not meager given suppositions such as the following: the principle of proportionate regard, God has attributes that can be expressed in novel ways via creation, all creaturely value is necessarily derived from God, and the like. The claim would not be that such suppositions entail that the only dominant motives God might have regarding creation are captured in glorificationism. Rather, the claim would be that such considerations reveal that the notion that God's creation-regarding acts would be dominantly (or fundamentally) motivated by self-glorification enjoys a decent prior probability. From there, the defender of glorificationism can claim that this prior probability coupled with glorificationism's great explanatory power makes glorificationism overall more probable than its contenders.

Such a probabilistic case might constitute a powerful way of arguing for glorificationism. But, of course, much of this case will depend upon the explanatory power of the view.

---

[1] Note: The Son *might* derive His value from the Father, given that He proceeds from the Father. If so, this would generate problems for this appeal to intra-trinitarian love, since given the motivational thesis, the Father would then love the Son primarily as an expression of self-love. Hence, not even the Father would love the Son in the relevantly rich manner.

The Explanatory Power of Glorificationism

Defenders of glorificationism often maintain that this perspective explains many passages of Scripture well. Some add that this explanatory power also extends to the problem of evil.

Regarding Scripture, Edwards (1989, 465–536) mounts a cumulative case for glorificationism. On the one hand, Edwards is right to highlight that glorificationism apparently explains numerous biblical passages well which ostensibly speak of God performing various actions for His own glory (e.g., Is. 43:7; Rom. 11:36). At the same time, it is difficult to derive glorificationism from Scripture. One reason for this comes from the fact that common discourse regarding reasons for action can be quite limited, if not outright misleading. Suppose that Axel says, "I am headed out to go to the store," and that in uttering this Axel reveals a purpose for collecting his keys and walking out to his car. From this utterance, it would be mistaken to assume that there isn't more to be said about why Axel is motivated to go to the store. It could be that Axel is going to the store to buy some wine for the purpose of entertaining guests, which is being done so that Axel might schmooze one of his guests in the hopes of securing a promotion at work, and it might be that Axel wants the promotion so that he can have the required income to expand his family comfortably. This artificial example illustrates that reasons for action are often considerably complex, and rarely do we delineate all the reasons we have for performing any given action, nor do we explain how the reasons relate one to another. What we often do is provide a reason that is sufficiently explanatory given the context. When you ask Axel why he is heading toward his car, the answer "I am going to the store" is enough. Unless you are a close friend, you would be confused if Axel answered the question "Why are you heading out?" with "So that Rose and I can have more kids!"

The elusive nature of ultimate reasons for acting is significant since glorificationism is a thesis that pertains to God's *ultimate* reason, or dominant motivation, for creating and governing the world. So, unless there are clues that the biblical passages under consideration concern God's ultimate reason for creating and interacting with the world, it's hasty to conclude from verses that speak of God glorifying Himself in various ways that this is evidence for glorificationism. It could be that God performs some self-glorifying action, not for its own sake, but as a means to something else. Or it could be that God performs a self-glorifying action for its own sake, but that this does not represent God's primary manner of dealing with creation.

Consider just one example. In Isaiah 43:7 God says that there is a people group "whom I created for my glory." We could very well understand this to mean that God has claimed a people for Himself (in this case Israel), so that God might be glorified among them for their good (Is. 43:1–4), and ultimately for the good of the entire world (e.g. Is. 42:1–7; Lk. 1:18–20; Jn. 12:32). Read in this way (which seems to be a plausible reading), God's self-glorification is subordinate to the goal of promoting the good of others. Hence, the passage provides no support for glorificationism. Yet this is the kind of passage on which Edwards bases his biblical case for glorificationism.

Of course, merely pointing out that it would be challenging to read glorificationism off the biblical texts does not show that glorificationism is not the best interpretation of Scripture overall. That would require a detailed discussion of the relevant biblical passages, which cannot be undertaken here. Nevertheless, one of the present authors has argued elsewhere (i.e., Wessling 2020a, 101–107) that there is at least one good theological reason to be skeptical that glorificationism represents the panoply of Scripture: glorificationism appears to contradict what Scripture teaches about the cruciform love of Christ.

Here's a summary of that argument. Glorificationism asserts that God is dominantly (or minimally fundamentally) motivated by self-expression. Plausibly, this entails that self-expression is the primary motive that guides God's central saving acts. If so, the implication is that God-in-Christ submitted Himself to crucifixion primarily motivated to express divine grace and other excellencies. Yet this is not what Scripture seems plainly to teach about why Christ allowed Himself to be crucified. Rather, it seems clear that Christ underwent the crucifixion primarily out of love for humanity (e.g., Rom 5:6-8; 2 Cor 8:9; Eph 5:1–2; Phil 2:3–8; 1 Jn 3:16; 1 Jn 4:7–11) and not primarily to glorify Himself or God the Father.

One line of evidence for this conclusion comes from the fact that Christ's self-giving love as demonstrated on the cross is upheld as an exemplary form of love that Christians should imitate in their love for others (e.g., Eph 5:1–2; Phil 2:3–8; 1 Jn 3:16; 1 Jn 4:7–11). But since it's ethically implausible to suppose that Christians are called to love others primarily motivated by self-interest or self-expression, it's implausible that Christ's motives for bearing the cross were similarly self-regarding. On the contrary, Christians are called in Phil 2:3-8 to put the interests of others above their own, in imitation of God-in-Christ's self-giving love and humility manifested most fully on the cross for humanity. Such motives stand in opposition to glorificationism, and so these considerations count strongly against the explanatory power of the glorificationist reading of Scripture.

Now consider the issue of God and evil. Some glorificationists have thought that this framework does a better job than others in explaining the existence of evil (e.g., Green 2016). By allowing various kinds of evil God can manifest certain attributes such as grace and retribution that would be impossible otherwise. Many add divine determinism to this and maintain that God causes whatever comes to pass for the sake of a greater good, which is the manifestation of divine glory. Sometimes this way of dealing with evil is also extended to explain why God sends some persons to hell (e.g., Calvin 1960, 3.24.14; Edwards 1997, 2001; Hart 2016).

Some find this schema for dealing with evil and hell satisfying, but others find it horrifying (see Pereboom 2005, 82; Baggett and Walls 2011, 74). Indeed, one might complain that such views call into question that it is good for all people for God to exist (see Vicens Forthcoming). One might also question whether this schema is compatible with biblical injunctions for all people to respond to God with what Brian Ballard calls "worshipful love" (2024). Additionally, even if one concedes that proponents of glorificationism can provide plausible rationalizations or just-so stories of various evils, it is doubtful that glorificationism *predicts* the evils we observe. It is not obvious, in other words, that we should expect a God motivated as the glorificationist postulates to allow manifold evils and forms of divine hiddenness to pervade our world. We won't attempt to solve such issues here. But whether the glorificationist takes on the noted auxiliary teachings or not, it seems that glorificationists have a considerable amount of work to do to show that it has great predictive power with respect to evil.

We have only scratched the surface of the issues related to glorificationism. But, from what we have examined, glorificationism does not look promising.

3 The Holiness Framework

In many religious traditions, God is understood to be holy. While there are several ways of understanding divine holiness (see Murphy 2021, 9–44 and Lebens 2024), the focus here is on holiness as a kind of separation from creation. A Holiness Framework, then, is any framework in which God is primarily motivated by considerations to keep some kind of separation or relational distance from creation. In this section, we examine a recent version of the Holiness Framework.

The Structure of the Holiness Framework

Although various religious traditions emphasize divine holiness, the interrelation between divine holiness and motives for divine action is rarely expounded upon. However, Mark C. Murphy rectifies this shortcoming in his book *Divine Holiness and Divine Action* (2021). He defends the Holiness Framework from a specifically Christian point of view. Since Murphy's Holiness Framework is the most detailed of its kind, we focus on it.

Murphy's Holiness Framework builds upon Rudolf Otto's influential work, *The Idea of the Holy* (1923). The borrowed core concept of this work is that experiences of the holy – that which is numinous, mysterious and other – comprise two features, the *fascinans* and *tremendum*. The holy is encountered as both extremely attractive (the *fascinans*) and as repulsive, or that which one is unfit to be in the presence of or to draw too close to (the *tremendum*). Murphy takes these features to be normative: one should experience the holy with both attraction and repulsion; this is what is merited by the relevant holy being. For God to be holy, then, is for God to possess those features that render appropriate a strong attraction to God by all creatures as well as a separation of these creatures from God. Moreover, Murphy argues that the God of Scripture ought to be conceived of as *absolutely* holy such that (a) it is impossible for there to be a rational creature for whom intimate union with God would not be supremely desirable, and (b) there will always be some level of intimate union with God for which that same creature is unfit. What makes various levels of intimate union with God unfitting is not merely that creatures are marred by sin (although that certainly contributes) but that they are limited in the value or goodness they possess, in contrast to God who enjoys unsurpassable worth.

Based on this idea of divine holiness, Murphy articulates a motivational framework for divine action. Important to this account is what Murphy (2021, esp. 112–113) labels *reasons of status*: those reasons possessed by agents, on account of their status rooted in some dimension of excellence or greatness, to keep from entering into numerous kinds of relationships with beings that are beneath this status (given their value, behavior, role, skills, or the like) within some context. Because God enjoys superlative value, God has motivating reasons of status to keep from entering various kinds of relationships with beings that are deficient, defective, or otherwise imperfect. God, in other words, recognizes the intrinsic value of the divine nature, realizes that He belongs in a class of His own, and is motivated by reasons concerning the objective misfit that comes with creatures being intimately united to Him. This Holiness Framework draws on the distinction between two kinds of reasons: *requiring reasons* versus (purely) *justifying reasons*. A requiring reason is a reason that an agent *must*, on pain of irrationality, act upon, provided that she does not also possess additional adequate reasons to do something else. By contrast, a merely justifying reason is a reason an agent *may* rationally act upon, so long as she does not also possess sufficient reason to the contrary. It might be said that requiring reasons provide rational *constraints* on action, whereas justifying reasons provide *opportunities* for rational action (Murphy 2021,

132–135). Finally, a *decisive reason* is a requiring reason to do some action that is unopposed by sufficiently weighty countervailing considerations.

According to Murphy's Holiness Framework, God has requiring reasons to respond to His own perfection by refraining from entering into various kinds of relationships with limited beings (i.e., creatures). The greater the limitations of the beings at issue and the more intimate the candidate relationship, the stronger God's requiring reasons are for refraining from entering into the relevant kind of relationship. Yet God still has reasons to act for our benefit and enter into various kinds of intimate relationships with us, which Murphy calls *reasons of love* (2021, 133). However, these reasons of love are always only justifying reasons and therefore do not necessitate divine action. So, God's reasons of love never are requiring reasons to advance human welfare, alleviate human suffering, or seek various kinds of union with humans.

Murphy mounts a comparative case for the Holiness Framework. Although not stated precisely in these terms, he contends that certain leading alternative frameworks have lower prior probabilities than the Holiness Framework (Murphy 2021, 79–125). Additionally, the Holiness Framework has greater explanatory power than other divine motivational frameworks, rendering it more probable on the whole than those alternative frameworks (e.g., Murphy 2021, 125–256). Both steps of the argument merit examination.

The Prior Probability of the Holiness Framework

Murphy compares his Holiness Framework with the Morality Framework discussed in Section 4 and a version of the Love Framework referenced in Section 5. To keep from repeating the material in these sections, we presently assess only those aspects of Murphy's arguments for the relatively high prior probability of the Holiness Framework that are not discussed elsewhere in this Element.

Consider, first, some background conditions that apparently provide evidence for the Holiness Framework. As indicated, Murphy draws from Otto's celebrated account of holiness, which relies heavily on the phenomenology of the holy. If one finds the borrowed aspects of Otto's phenomenological analysis of the holy to be an apt description of things, this may be counted toward the prior probability of the Holiness Framework. This is because this phenomenological data is part of the background knowledge that is independent of the framework's ability to explain divine action as found in the salvation arc of Scripture and in relation to evil and hiddenness. Although some find the relevant phenomenological analysis in need of either abandonment (Yadav 2023) or augmentation (e.g., Cuneo and Strabbing 2023), perhaps many find the basic analysis plausible as well. For those with this latter judgment, this analysis counts in favor of the Holiness Framework.

Another background consideration on behalf of the Holiness Framework concerns the aforementioned reasons of status. Without overlooking complications related to ways in which one can appeal to status as an abuse of power, Murphy observes that we commonly think that reasons of status provide persons with reason not to enter or remain in certain kinds of relationships. In order to evoke this intuition, Murphy considers a statement from David Foster Wallace that his playing tennis with Michael Joyce (a professional tennis player) would be "absurd and in a certain way obscene" on account of the fact that it would be unbefitting of Joyce's talent to engage in such a condescending mismatch (2021, 115). Similarly, Murphy claims, "When presumptuous young men challenge professional women's basketball players to games of one-on-one [...], these women are simply correct to note that the gap between their excellence and these young men's skills is such that it is beneath these women to play them" (2021, 117). Examples such as these fund Murphy's argument that "If even between two humans, both finite creatures of roughly equal physical and mental powers, there can be reasons of status in some contexts, reasons that both parties to the relationship should acknowledge, then *a fortiori* there will be those reasons with respect to the relationship between God and humans" (118).

One might push back against Murphy's account by considering its apparently implausible implications (see Cuneo and Strabbing 2023, 415–416). For instance, Murphy's use of reasons of status seems to entail that it is unfitting for beings of great value to be united to beings of much less value in ways which include engaging in shared projects, being emotionally connected, or enjoying each other's company. But if this principle holds, then you would have a requiring reason not to engage with and enjoy the company of a hummingbird that visits the cherry blossoms outside your window, due to the value gap between humans and hummingbirds. Yet, *contra* Murphy, there does not seem to be any such requiring reason.

To circumvent such problems, Cuneo and Strabbing (2023, 416) propose an alternative to Murphy's account of status reasons. They maintain that "what makes something a status reason for A to refrain from $j$ing in a given context is not just the value gap between A and B, but that $j$ing would express something untrue about the value gap, namely, that there is no such gap (or that the gap is much smaller than it is)." Thus, insofar as relating to creation in numerous intimate ways does not express something untrue about the value gap between God and creation, God has no requiring reasons of status not to forge such intimate relationships with creation. What *does* give God reason to keep His distance is creaturely sin. Since humans, for instance, are prone to mistreat God,

God has reasons of status not to enter intimate relationships with sinful creatures on account of God's moral goodness.

Murphy responds to this objection by maintaining that God, unlike in the case of inter-creaturely relations, always has reason to keep distance from creatures, given the vast value-gulf that exists between God and creatures (2023, 476–477). Moreover, Murphy agrees with Cuneo and Strabbing that God has especially strong reasons to refrain from intimate relationships with sinful creatures. However, since Murphy denies that God is a conventional moral agent, he does not believe these avoidance-related reasons come from divine moral goodness. Rather, God has especially strong requiring reasons to keep distance from sinners because sin is an especially horrendous creaturely limitation, one that is *against* the good.

A different challenge to Murphy's account of reasons of status is that God's superior value does not obviously imply that intimate union with creatures would be unfitting (Yadav 2023, 462–463). There are, after all, instances in which differential value is normative to relationships, where a mismatch in skill, excellence, and the like are the basis of these relationships (e.g., a professor with a student or a professional tennis player offering beginner lessons). Perhaps humans stand in such a relationship to God, where the value differential does not call God to keep distance.

Murphy is unpersuaded (2023, 477). He grants that there are normative inequality-entailing relationships. Nonetheless, there can be inequalities that are so great that they give those with a certain status requiring reason not to get entangled in relationships that exemplify such inequalities. For example, there are lazy, incapable, and disinterested students that *qua* students are simply beneath the status of certain expert professors. The presence of this reality partly explains why we admire it when gifted instructors are willing to forgo other opportunities to work with unusually difficult students. Murphy holds that all creatures stand in a similar relation to God, only extraordinarily amplified. All creatures are so far beneath God as to give God requiring reasons to keep distance.

In our judgment, it is unclear on a priori grounds alone whether Murphy or his interlocutors are right about reasons of status. If this judgment is on the mark, the prior probability of the Holiness Framework is adversely affected.

However, Murphy does not want to argue simply that the prior probability of the Holiness Framework is reasonably high. He wants to make the stronger claim that the Holiness Framework has a higher prior probability than the Morality and Love Frameworks.

The proponent of the Morality Framework maintains that God perfectly conforms to a set of moral norms that, minimally, are analogous to the norms that characteristically apply to human behavior. Against this framework, Murphy (2017, 22–66; 2021, 79–108) contends that there is a strong basis for maintaining that the moral norms that bind humans do not necessarily bind God, and thus God should not be conceived as a conventional moral agent. A significant plank in Murphy's case is the claim that creatures (including humans) do not enjoy intrinsic value. The denial of such value to creatures comes in the context of considering what might ground divine requiring reasons to promote and protect creaturely well-being. If God does not have such reasons, then we can conclude that God is not a moral agent of the kind essential for the Morality Framework.

However, it is unlikely that Murphy's argument against creaturely intrinsic value is successful (see Rubio Forthcoming). But if that is so, Murphy has a second line of defense (2023, 480). Even if creatures are intrinsically valuable in some sense, it remains the case that creatures have the wrong kind of value to generate requiring reasons for God. Creatures are good only by participation, by derivation or reflection of divine goodness. But it is doubtful that a goodness that is entirely derivative or reflective of God's goodness would subject God to requiring reasons to promote and protect that creaturely value (see Murphy 2017, 60–62; Murphy 2021, 95).

We don't share Murphy's confidence in this judgment. Consider two alternatives. It might be that, since God possesses all values within His own being, God finds Himself with only justifying and not requiring reasons to promote and protect creaturely well-being. This is how Murphy assesses things. Yet it might be that, because God values Himself, He values that which genuinely participates in the goodness He antecedently values, and this gives God requiring reasons to promote and protect the creatures that are relevantly valued. It might be that what makes love of the divine nature fitting transfers (in part or whole) to love of those creatures who are bearers of some facet of the divine beauty (cf. Adams 1999, 177–198; Rutledge and Wessling 2023, 441–442), which corresponds with the relevant kinds of requiring reasons. It is difficult to judge on a priori grounds which of these alternatives are closer to the truth. Because of this, we don't share Murphy's confidence in the judgment at issue. Hence, it seems that we cannot conclude from such a consideration that there is a higher prior probability to the notion that God has only justifying reason to promote and protect creaturely well-being, even if we cannot conclude that the probabilities swing in the opposite direction either.

Another response to Murphy's argument is to deny that all creaturely value is derived from God via participation/reflection. If the exemplarist doctrine of divine ideas described in Section 2 holds, there is a sense in which all value finds its source in God, yet creaturely value is not relevantly derived from God.

According to this doctrine, creatures are valuable in virtue of exactly resembling some facet of God. If this is how creatures are valuable, it's plausible that the reasons that God has for valuing those aspects of Himself transfer (in part or whole) to creatures. Although it is unclear that such a setup would entail that God has requiring reasons to promote and protect human welfare, neither can one simply close the door on this possibility. Hence, exemplarism plausibly not only undercuts Murphy's case against creaturely intrinsic value but also diminishes the force of Murphy's considerations on behalf of the idea that God doesn't have requiring reasons to promote and protect human welfare.

In our judgment, the crux of Murphy's case against the Morality Framework concerns his exploitation of the logical gap that exists between *the goodness of the promotion and protection of someone's well-being* and *one having requiring reasons to promote or protect said person's well-being*. Philosophers have long noticed this gap and have proposed various explanatory theories as to why humans generally should tend to the welfare of others. Such theories include Hobbesian, Humean, Aristotelian, and Kantian accounts. Importantly, though, none of these accounts or other leading alternatives, even if successful in shedding light on human moral requirements, gives us good reason to think that God would similarly have decisive reason to tend to the welfare of creatures. Quite the contrary, if any of these views are successful at explaining why the welfare of others provides humans with reasons for action, then "we thereby have a powerful basis for *denying* that an absolutely perfect being must have decisive reason to promote and protect the well-being of us creatures" (Murphy 2021, 93).

A number of responses have been given to this argument from Murphy.

Some merely attempt to weaken the force of Murphy's contention. They argue that the supposition that *the reasons humans have for promoting/protecting human well-being do not apply to God* gives us insufficient cause to doubt that God might have His own decisive reasons for such moral action (Cuneo and Strabbing 2023, 421–422; Rutledge and Wessling 2023, 445–446). After all, an individual having several independent requiring reasons to act is commonplace (say, because it contributes to her flourishing, because God has commanded it, because her role as a parent requires it, or because she would be liable to criminal charges were she not to perform the relevant action). Given that we are well-acquainted with this phenomenon, the supposition that *the reasons humans have for moral action do not apply to God* perhaps only gives us modest grounds to doubt that God could have His own (requiring) reasons to promote/ protect human well-being. So, perhaps we should look elsewhere – say, to Scripture or Christian tradition – to determine whether God has decisive reasons to act in this manner.

Alternatively, one might highlight the apparently untoward theological implications of Murphy's vision of God. If God has no requiring reason to promote and protect human welfare, God could in principle be motivated to perform frightfully cruel actions (Wielenberg 2017; Ekstrom 2021, 156–187). This appears not just unsettling but mistaken, since God's creation of humans seems to embed God within a nexus of requiring reasons related to protecting and promoting human welfare (e.g., Hadsell Unpublished; Satta 2020). For example, God stands in something analogous to a parent relation to humanity, which ostensibly makes Him responsible for us in certain (requiring) respects.

Chris Tucker (2020) objects to Murphy's argument by providing an independently plausible account of the interrelation between reasons and value wherein God has requiring reasons to promote and protect human well-being. Since Tucker's proposal will reappear in Section 5, it is worth presenting it here in some detail.

Tucker gives an account of a human's life being *fully good*. Roughly, a human's life is fully good if it possesses all the goods that her nature is designed to have to flourish, both on the whole and in every part of this life. A fully good life rarely, if ever, requires maximization of the relevant goods. Humans require a certain degree of intelligence, but there is nothing about human nature that requires maximal intelligence or even three times the IQ of Einstein to live fully well, even if maximal intelligence or the higher IQ would be much better. Similarly, suppose humans ought to have at least one unit of pleasure at each moment of their existence. Although ten units of pleasure at each moment presumably would be better, a fully good human life does not require it. Such increases would constitute only quantitative adjustments to the qualities that make some human's life fully good.

If human lives can be fully good, there are three basic axiological states that humans can have in relation to their well-being. They can have (i) a fully good life, or (ii) a life that exceeds the fully good, or (iii) a life that falls short of the fully good. Given this, what kinds of reasons might God have to bring about these three different states? Murphy contends that God has only justifying reasons to bring about any of the three. But Tucker notices that we expect qualitative axiological differences to correlate with qualitative normative differences. In other words, we expect the differences in the quality of human lives realizable by God to correlate with different kinds of reasons for divine action. For illustration, suppose that an ethicist is committed to the idea that humans are the only terrestrial creature to enjoy intrinsic dignity and that this dignity makes humans significantly and qualitatively more valuable than nonhuman animals. Given such a commitment, one would expect the ethicist to maintain that human dignity generates special normative treatment. All other things being equal, an ethical theory is preferable to the extent that its normative and axiological commitments cohere or fit together nicely. But then it seems strange that God would have only justifying reasons to bring about the three mentioned states regarding human well-being. For a merely fully good human life is qualitatively different from a life that falls short of it.

A better normative-axiological fit would be as follows. God has requiring reason to bring about merely fully good human lives, but only justifying reasons to ensure that human lives exceed the merely fully good. This is a better normative-axiological fit than the one proposed by Murphy because the kinds of normative reasons postulated for God account for the differences in the axiological landscape. Since adding to a fully good life is a quantitative rather than a qualitative difference, it makes sense that God would have merely justifying reasons to bring about that which exceeds a fully good human life. Similarly, because the possession of a fully good human life is qualitatively better than a human life that falls short of the fully good, it makes sense to suppose that God would have requiring reasons to bring about the former. And if God sometimes has unopposed requiring reasons to bring about merely fully good human lives, then God sometimes has decisive reasons to bring about these good states of affairs. If that is so, then Murphy's argument against the Morality Framework is undercut.

In our judgment, Tucker's proposal captures the relevant normative-axiological fit more naturally than Murphy's. Plus, there are the other concerns with Murphy's view noted previously: (i) Murphy's argument from the logical gap between the goodness of someone's well-being and a human having requiring reason to promote/protect it unreliably detects whether God would have the relevant decisive reasons, (ii) the conclusion of this logical gap argument leads to untoward theological implications, and (iii) intuitions about God's creation of humans generating the relevant requiring reasons count against Murphy's view. Tucker's proposal combined with these other considerations plausibly outweighs Murphy's case against the Morality Framework.

But how does the Holiness Framework compare with the Love Framework? Since we examine the Love Framework subsequently, we will not summarize Murphy's case against it here. Suffice it to say that, in our estimation, many of Murphy's critiques of the versions of the Love Framework he discusses are strong (see Murphy 2017, 22–44, and 2021, 98–108). Hence, Murphy plausibly demonstrates that his Holiness Framework has a higher prior probability than them. Yet we maintain that the Agapist Framework defended in Sections 5 and 6 constitutes a different version of the Love Framework that eludes Murphy's criticisms (even if it must answer Murphy's challenges to the Morality Framework).

What, then, should we make of the prior probability of the Holiness Framework as defended by Murphy? We judge that the prior probability of the Holiness Framework is higher than glorificationism since it does not inherit similar liabilities as the latter framework as discussed in Section 2. Additionally, the kinds of considerations Murphy offers succeed in showing that the Holiness Framework has a higher prior probability than the versions of the Love Framework he discusses and does not suffer from a substantially lower prior probability than the Morality Framework. Whether Murphy succeeds in demonstrating that the Holiness Framework has a prior probability that is equal to or higher than the Morality Framework will greatly depend upon one's assessment of the effectiveness of Murphy's aforementioned exploitation of the logical gap concerning human well-being and God's reasons to promote/protect it. We leave the final adjudication of this matter to the reader, but for the reasons indicated, we maintain the Holiness Framework is slightly beneath the Morality Framework on this score (see also Sections 4 and 6). Now we turn to an assessment of the explanatory power of the Holiness Framework.

The Explanatory Power of the Holiness Framework

Murphy maintains that the Holiness Framework predicts various biblical themes and Christian doctrines and avoids the evidential force of standard statements of the problems of evil and divine hiddenness. Consider these in turn.

The Holiness Framework is said to accord with (i) scriptural declarations that God is absolutely holy, (ii) depictions of God appealing to His own holiness to explain His actions, especially in keeping distance from the unclean, defiled, and impure, and (iii) instances of God calling created persons to behave in certain ways which exemplify moralistic and ritualistic holiness (Murphy 2021, 126–132). Such things are predicted with the Holiness Framework, although Murphy is well aware that Scripture underdetermines which divine motivational framework is correct (2021, 126, 132).

Murphy's evaluation of the biblical material has been met with mixed reactions. Sameer Yadav (2023, 463, n. 11) contends that Murphy is mistaken in following those who treat the Hebrew *qdš* as having a basic meaning of "separateness" and maintain that "holy" and "impure" are semantic opposites. Rather, Yadav draws from the work of David Clines (2021) to suggest *qdš* is more reliably read as indicating that which God has uniquely made His possession and thereby has come to associate with Himself. Thus, *qdš* is nearly the opposite of the separateness reading adopted by Murphy. Yadav (2023, 460) furthermore contends that the biblical picture emphasizes that it is creaturely sinfulness, not limitations of value as such, which drive God to separate from creatures.

Fleischacker (2023) contrasts Murphy's handling of the biblical material with one that he develops in conversation with the Jewish theological tradition (cf. Lebens 2024). Like Murphy, Fleischacker understands holiness to have to do with separateness. However, Fleischacker maintains that God separates Himself from humans for our sake, enabling us to see all of creation as belonging to the Creator and revealing something of the mysterious divine personality.

Murphy has responded to these objections (2023, 473–475 and 478). Part of his biblical case for the Holiness Framework – which is indebted to significant Old Testament scholarship – is that the holiness code in Leviticus depicts God as keeping His distance from us on account of our creatureliness, that is, on account of the fact that we decay and die and need to procreate to continue our kind. Hence it is not simply sin or space for revealing the divine personality that puts the unlimitedly excellent God at a remove from us. It is rather our limitedness.

But even if one agrees with Murphy that divine holiness should be understood in terms of separation from our limitedness, for the Holiness framework to be supported by the Old Testament witness, divine holiness must be presented as motivationally more fundamental than other divine attributes. Yet this is unclear. Arguably, the key description of the divine character in the Old Testament is found in Yahweh's declaration to Moses in Exodus 34:6 that He is "a God merciful and gracious, slow to anger, and abounding in steadfast love and faithfulness ... " So, divine mercy, grace, and love may be judged more motivationally fundamental than holiness. Corroboration for this judgment about the divine character in the Old Testament comes from the way that the content of Yahweh's declaration to Moses is cited elsewhere as an apparently key description of God (Num. 14:18; 2 Chr. 30:9; Neh. 9:17; Ps. 86:15; 103:8; 111:4; 112:4; 116:5; 145:8; Joel 2:13).

In terms of the New Testament witness, we arguably find Jesus advocating for an understanding of God *principally* in terms of compassion and transforming love (see Borg 1998, 88–151). One example of this evidence comes in the climax of the Sermon on the Plain, where Jesus replaces the injunction "You shall be holy, for I the Lord your God am holy" (Lev. 19:2) with "Be compassionate [or merciful], just as your Father is compassionate" (Luke 6:36). Though God is rightly understood to be holy, this holiness does not (primarily) inspire God to keep distance from humanity. In Christ we rather find that God is fundamentally motivated by a love and mercy that leads Him to abide with sinners. Although there are ways in which proponents of the Holiness

Framework can account for Jesus's presentation of God, it sits uncomfortably with this framework.

With respect to Christian doctrines, Murphy offers many desiderata for which the Holiness Framework accounts. Among them is the idea that the Holiness Framework excellently explains the contingency of creation (2021, 137–148). This is because, unlike the Love and Morality Frameworks which incline toward necessitarianism regarding creation, God doesn't create anything by default on the Holiness Framework. Creating is necessarily the sort of action that is beneath God's status, since God would be directly present to all of creation as He sustains it in existence. This is an intimate kind of relationship that the holy God has strong requiring reason to avoid. But God, on Murphy's view, has justifying reasons of love to create. Creation is thus contingent.

Something similar is true of the Incarnation, according to Murphy (2021, 161–187). Murphy argues that the Incarnation is utterly surprising and normatively weird, and the Holiness Framework explains this well. Two features of the Holiness Framework illuminate why this is so: "first, the overwhelming strength of the requiring reasons that God has against assuming a human nature, and second, that the reasons of love on which God is acting are justifying only and deeply disproportionate to the reasons of absolute holiness." So, "we should expect that such a [holy] God would refrain from becoming incarnate" (Murphy 2021, 169).

Next, consider the atonement. For Murphy (2021, 188–211), one key point of the atonement is that God wants to deal with an obstacle to the *fittingness* of His union with human persons – that is, an obstacle grounded in the fact that humans have sinned. Whatever the mechanism of atonement is, it somehow removes or lessens the obstacle to union in a manner that attends to the importance of God's holiness. Murphy takes the fact that Christ's atoning work addresses issues of fittingness for union to favor the Holiness Framework over its alternatives.

Finally, consider eschatology. Murphy (2021, 218–235) argues that the Holiness Framework explains the possibility of everlasting damnation better than alternative frameworks. He maintains that God's holiness might require him to withdraw from confirmed sinners, leaving them in their self-imposed sinful condition forever. Frameworks that place a premium on weighty requiring reasons of divine love apparently do not have similarly available resources.

What the Holiness Framework is said to explain is more expansive and nuanced than can be discussed presently. However, it seems clear that the Holiness Framework is at a comparative disadvantage in predicting certain key theological desiderata. For instance, if God's default is to keep His distance, then, by Murphy's own admission, creation, Incarnation, atonement by bloody death, and intimate eschatological blessedness are each rather surprising. By contrast, divine motivational frameworks which place an emphasis on love predict these outcomes to a high degree (see Rutledge and Wessling 2023; Wynn 2022, 64).

Murphy (2023, 483–484) counters this kind of challenge by maintaining that it targets the wrong explanandum. In Murphy's view, we do not want a divine motivational framework that simply predicts that God will create, become incarnate and all the rest. Rather, we want a framework that explains why God does these things *when it is very surprising that He would do them*. For "Scripture and the common practice of the Church has treated divine action as wondrous in this way" (Murphy 2023, 484). There is an added layer of complexity here for which the Holiness Framework accounts.

This response largely hangs on the normative surprisingness of God's generous acts. On Murphy's Holiness Framework, creation, the Incarnation, the costly atonement, and intimate heavenly blessedness themselves are each independently unexpected and normatively surprising. The collective is plausibly taken to be exponentially more unexpected on the Holiness Framework. If a motivational framework can predict these actions and yet maintain some sense of the wonder and surprise that God has performed them, such a framework would have a significant advantage over Murphy's Holiness Framework (compare Cuneo & Strabbing 2023, 417–418, with Murphy 2023, 484–485).

With this in mind, consider the reflections from Richard Swinburne on how initial surprise may ultimately dovetail with the available evidence. While arguing that the Resurrection of Christ is not improbable given certain background considerations, Swinburne writes:

> When I give these reasons, the reader will be right to feel that I would not have given them if I had not derived them from the Christian tradition [...] [We need] the Christian tradition to make us aware of a theory – a particular theory of the divine nature and of what a being with that nature might be expected to do [...] – before we can judge whether or not, by objective standards, the evidence supports that theory well. Most physicists could never have invented the general theory of relativity for themselves, but once it has been proposed for discussion, they can assess whether in fact the evidence supports it. [...] But the evidential relations were there, whether or not they saw them. I shall be arguing that the Christian tradition of what God might be expected to do is correct. (Swinburne 2003, 35)

We might describe Swinburne's basic idea as follows. No philosophical theologian, however bright, would be able to predict justifiably, apart from knowledge of the Christian tradition, that God would become incarnate and atone for sins in the wonderful manner affirmed by Christians. In that sense, the Christian salvation story is immensely surprising. But once one sees the whole

Christian picture of things, including the fact that the triune God is intensely loving, one can discern that the resurrection of Christ is not improbable given the character of the Christian God.

Murphy locates the surprisingness of God's creation and redemption in the motivational structure of God. This is disputable. Many Christians have thought that God is disposed toward creating and redeeming humans (see van Driel 2008). These Christians might therefore locate the relevant surprisingness in *us*, in our inability to predict the ways of God without the clearer picture afforded by special revelation. But once we become acquainted with the claims of Christian revelation, we can discern that the glorious salvation story is expected given God's character.

One reason to favor this second way of making sense of the relevant surprise factor is that it allows individuals to opt for a framework that is more securely confirmed than the Holiness Framework by the aforementioned theological desiderata. For, again, the Holiness Framework renders it objectively probable that God would not create, nor become Incarnate, nor atone in a bloody human-identifying manner, nor save humans via intimate heavenly union. But, all things being equal, it seems better to adopt a divine motivational framework where these divine actions are not collectively improbable and yet accounts for the wonderful surprisingness of such actions.

Interestingly, Murphy's Holiness Framework upends contemporary convictions about what God would be expected to do. On this framework it is unsurprising that God would allow evil and remain hidden. Since God is absolutely holy, God's default setting is not to be intimately involved with creation, especially when it has gone awry. So, while God would never intend evil (since God's reasons are responsive to what is good), "there should be no general expectation that God would eliminate gratuitous evils, and God may even have a reason not to combat evils" (Murphy 2021, 137). Similarly, God has requiring reasons of status to avoid entering into intimate relationships with creatures. Hence, a decision by God to remain hidden from some or all creatures is unsurprising. It's rather to be expected (Murphy 2021, 155). In these ways, Murphy's Holiness Framework reverses the way in which contemporary philosophers and theologians have come to think about what God might do.

Some argue that this reversal of expectations calls into question the worship-worthiness of God (Mariña 2021, 197; Yadav 2023, 466–468), and others question whether it would be good for humans were such a God to exist (Vicens Forthcoming). The jury remains out on these issues.

However, the Holiness Framework plausibly mitigates the problems of evil and divine hiddenness, which counts in its favor. Yet the advantages the Holiness Framework has on this score should not be overstated.

On the Holiness Framework, God has only justifying reasons to advance and protect human welfare. What would the weight of these justifying reasons be? It's difficult to say. However, assuming that there should be a normative-axiological fit as previously discussed, it seems that, *minimally*, God would have fairly weighty justifying reasons to bring about merely fully good human lives, assuming that there are such lives and that they constitute a significant qualitative change within the axiological landscape. Furthermore, one suspects that weighty reasons concerning human welfare would, ceteris paribus, incline (without requiring) God to act accordingly. Why think God would be so inclined on Murphy's divine motivational framework? Because Murphy holds that God is perfectly rational and free, and thus that God's agency is entirely explained by His assessment of the reasons to act and not on the basis of brute preferences or desires (Murphy 2017, 27). But then it looks like God generally would be disposed to protect and promote human welfare (including overcoming certain kinds of divine hiddenness) given the presence of the relevant weighty reasons, the absence of any nonrational influence on divine action, and the absence of countervailing considerations. While Murphy can point to holiness reasons as countervailing considerations for God not to promote and protect human welfare, it remains the case that God has significant justifying reasons to eliminate evil and suffering – reasons which God may act upon. By contrast, there is no force behind nature that has reasons for such elimination if naturalism is true. If this is right, the Holiness Framework presents a vision of theism that still seems to be at a comparable disadvantage with naturalism in explaining the depth and scope of human suffering (see Wilson 2024).

Of course, the Holiness Framework's being at a disadvantage vis-à-vis naturalism concerning evil does not preclude the Holiness Framework from having an advantage over competing motivational frameworks in explaining evil. For, unlike its competitors, the Holiness Framework postulates that God has weighty requiring reasons of holiness not to get entangled with the world's evils. Plus, proponents of the Holiness Framework may utilize standard theodicies and defenses (Murphy 2021, 148–153). But the more one amplifies the weight of God's holiness reasons to explain why God does not rectify evils, the more surprising the salvation arc of Christian Scripture becomes. In other words, evil is explained at the cost of making God's creation and deeply loving redemption of the world unexpected, even out of character in some sense. This is a substantial theological cost, which significantly weakens the explanatory scope and power of the Holiness Framework. In our judgment, the cost is sufficient to merit looking to alternative motivational frameworks.

4 The Morality Framework

One of the most significant frameworks for divine motivation, especially among contemporary philosophers of religion, is the Morality Framework. According to it, God's creation-directed motives perfectly conform to moral norms. These moral norms are often understood to be similar to those embedded in leading normative ethical systems, such as deontology, consequentialism, virtue theory, or some combination thereof (see Hoffman and Rosenkrantz 2002, 143–165; Garcia 2009). So, the proponent of the Morality Framework might say that what fundamentally drives God to do what He does in relation to humans is fulfilling various obligations that God has, and/or maximizing human welfare, and/or exemplifying perfect virtue, and the like. Beneath the surface, then, is the supposition that God is morally good in some sense analogous to human moral goodness (see, e.g., Morris 1987, 43; Garcia 2009; Murphy 2017, 23–29, and 2019, Section 1). Consequently, proponents of the Morality Framework regularly assume that God's fundamental creation-directed motives conform perfectly to moral norms that are generally comparable to those that should direct human behavior.

In this section we survey arguments for and against the Morality Framework. We shall find that this framework constitutes a plausible divine motivational framework, worthy of serious consideration. This is significant since the Agapist Framework defended in subsequent sections plausibly is a version of the Morality Framework, one that provides a more detailed understanding of divine motivation.

The Prior Probability of the Morality Framework

The Morality Framework naturally emerges when two widespread convictions are held alongside the notion of God as morally perfect. The first is that morality places certain unavoidable expectations or imperatives on its subjects. In other words, the norms of morality provide reasons for action that cannot be ignored with full immunity, and perhaps cannot be ignored with rational consistency (see Murphy 2017, 25–27). The second conviction is that moral norms nearly always inform how one ought to treat others. Taken together, the idea is that a morally perfect God necessarily follows moral norms when they bear upon God's actions, and these moral norms almost always inform how God ought to treat others, including humans.

Given these two widespread convictions, the Morality Framework may be said to have a decently high prior probability if it can be shown that there is good antecedent reason to suppose that God is morally perfect. The working assumption of many is that God enjoys such perfection. Here are just a few statements from contemporary philosophers: "It is a matter of consensus that God is perfectly morally good" (Peterson, et al. 2013, 147); "Theists believe that God is perfectly morally good" (Layman 2022, 1); "Theists hold that God is absolutely and perfectly good ... God is taken to be not merely morally faultless, but morally unsurpassable" (Murray and Rea 2008, 26).

Some maintain divine moral perfection follows from other divine attributes. One might argue, for instance, that moral goodness follows from omniscience, perfect freedom, and omnipotence, given moral objectivism and a certain account of moral reasons (see Swinburne 2004, 99–105). Begin with the idea that an omniscient being would recognize all the reasons there are for performing some act, while a perfectly free agent would be motivated to act only upon the weight of these reasons rather than upon irrational desires, sensuous impulses, and so on. Add to this that morally good actions, or minimally morally obligatory ones, necessarily come with all-things-considered reasons to do them and that bad or morally impermissible actions necessarily come with all-things-considered reasons against doing them. Moreover, since some moral principles and obligations are necessarily true, plausibly these principles and obligations apply to all rational agents, including God. So, given omniscience and perfect freedom, God always knows which actions are good or obligatory (what He has all-things-considered reasons to do) and which actions He must not do (what God has all-things-considered reasons not to do) and He is necessarily motivated to act accordingly. If God is omnipotent, furthermore, God is always able to accomplish what He is motivated to do. From this one might further deduce that if God is necessarily predisposed to do that which is good and avoid that which is bad, God is necessarily morally virtuous as well.

Unfortunately, it is unclear that this is a successful argument against those who doubt that God is conventionally moral. What this argument shows is that God would be necessarily disposed to perform morally good actions and avoid bad ones *if* God is subject to moral norms (Murphy 2021, 87–89; Wilson 2022, 38–51). But even if we grant that some moral principles are necessary, this does not show that God is subject to them. It may be that these necessary moral principles only apply to particular beings, for example humans. The utility of this argument, we think, is that it supports the thought that *if* God is subject to moral norms, then God is not merely moral but morally perfect.

Another common way of arriving at the position that God is morally perfect is via the method of perfect being theology. As mentioned in Section 1, proponents of perfect being theology claim that maximal perfection or greatness is central to elucidating the concept of God. From there, one can argue that it is better to be morally perfect than not (that it's a pure perfection), and so this provides reason to think that the absolutely perfect being, God, is morally perfect (see Rogers 2000, 120–135; Hill 2005, 192–227).

The trouble is that some find themselves without the intuition that a maximally perfect being must be a moral being. There are also objections to this notion. One might therefore argue that the proponent of the Morality Framework should propose evidence, beyond this appeal to intuition, for the claim that a maximally perfect being must be a moral one (Murphy 2017, 62).

While it is certainly preferable to have additional evidence for the notion that God is morally perfect, intuitions are arguably a kind of evidence. If so, then those who find themselves with the strong intuition that morality goes all the way up, as it were, to a morally perfect God have at least some grounds for supposing the relevant conception of God is true.

Here is a related reason to affirm the high prior probability of divine moral perfection. Theists almost always hold that God is worthy of worship and total devotion. But, plausibly, a necessary condition of what makes individuals intrinsically appropriate objects of praise and devotion is moral goodness. When it comes to the worship of God, "only a morally perfect being could be worthy of the unqualified devotion typical of theistic worship" (Quinn 1992, 289). Hence the morality framework seems supported by this deep-seated conviction about God being worthy of worship and devotion.

However, this argument from worship-worthiness has been challenged. Murphy argues that a being is worthy of a person's worship if "there is a massive inequality between that being and that person, and the inequality is an inequality of a certain sort of value" (2017, 130). He thinks that God can fulfill the second requirement on the basis of other great-making properties besides moral perfection, thereby undermining the derivation. In saying this, Murphy acknowledges that a God who transcends morality would not necessarily be allegiance-worthy (2017, 133–134).

But, *pace* Murphy, submission, surrender, subservience, obeisance, and allegiance (Kvanvig 2021, 25–27) seem central to the worship of the supremely worship-worthy God. Given this, Kvanvig rightly maintains that "to be supremely worthy of the highest worship requires divine goodness, since a lack of such would support qualifications in the attitude of worship" (2021, 170). Otherwise put, one can rationally choose to entrust oneself in worshipful-allegiance to God unqualifiedly only if God is perfectly moral in the manner that can be counted on to have one's best interests in mind (*pace* Rea 2022) – in a word, supremely trustworthy. Although an argument of this kind rests upon contentious premises, the premises are reasonable, especially for those who take worship-worthiness as essential to who God is and a key starting point for theologizing (see Kvanvig 2021, *passim*).

A final reason to affirm that God is morally perfect comes from the idea that God is the foundation of morality. The argument could go like this. God is perfectly morally virtuous. All creaturely moral virtues are such because they resemble or participate in God's virtues (e.g., Zagzebski 2004). Some might add that moral obligations are also nonarbitrarily legislated by God since they come from one that is unsurpassable in moral virtue (e.g., Jordan 2012, 55–56; Loke 2023, 33–34). A similar line of reasoning for the moral perfection of God is this: God is The Good, hence the standard of each species of goodness, including moral goodness (see Leftow 2006, 369–375). The inference then would be that God as the standard of moral goodness is perfectly moral.

These enumerated considerations depend upon contested notions that cannot be examined here. Nonetheless, the arguments from perfect being theology, supreme worship-worthiness, and God as morality's foundation arguably provide some indication that the Morality Framework has a reasonably high prior probability, at least for those that share the relevant commitments. But there are direct challenges to the prior probability of the Morality Framework that its defenders must overcome.

Much discussed challenges of this kind to the Morality Framework include objections related to the inability of God to have the right kind of freedom to be necessarily morally praiseworthy (e.g., Alston 1990; cf. Stump 1992; Morriston 2000; Leftow 2013, 88–90 and Howard-Snyder 2017; cf. Couenhoven 2016 and Timpe 2016a and 2016b), the impossibility of exemplifying moral perfection (e.g., Conee 1994; Rowe 2003; cf. Leftow 2013, 74–78 and Murphy 2019, Section 4), and features about God's nature that preclude Him from possessing moral virtues or being subject to obligation-generating contexts (à la Davies 2006 and 2011; cf. Leftow 2013). However, to our minds, the force of these objections has been largely undercut. For reasons of space, therefore, we here focus on challenges to the prior probability of the Morality Framework that remain more pressing.

First, some question whether God would always act upon His moral reasons. Perhaps God sometimes needs to choose between moral and nonmoral values (e.g., aesthetic value) that are incommensurate or "on a par" (in the sense given by Chang 2002). God would then not be rationally required to select the moral option in such cases (e.g., Draper 2019). If this view is plausible, it cuts against the prior probability of the Morality Framework, since we would not have assurance that God must be fundamentally motivated by moral norms.

In response, the claim that God might be forced to choose between moral and nonmoral values requires that God could be faced with this kind of situation. But in what situation would the omnipotent and omniscient God be forced to choose between acting morally toward creatures and, say, creating great beauty?

Draper (2019) gives the example of God's answer to Job appealing to the aesthetic majesty of creation in response to the charge that God has acted unjustly. But couldn't God create a beautiful world *and* act perfectly morally toward creatures?

A stronger response on behalf of the Morality Framework consists in denying that God could ever violate moral obligations (this could be reframed in terms of a divine virtue ethic; see, e.g., Alston 1990). For, as mentioned, moral obligations by definition cannot be ignored responsibly. There are many arguments that could be given for this position. Here is one. It seems appropriate to blame agents for violating (all-things-considered) moral obligations. But if an agent could have nonmoral reasons that justify violating these obligations, then blame would be inappropriate (Murphy 2017, 26; cf. Elmore 2024). Here is another. It seems that once I become convinced that I have a moral obligation concerning an action, further deliberation is unnecessary. Once it's settled that one has a moral obligation, deliberation ought to come to an end. But this would not be the case if it is possible for nonmoral reasons to justify violating moral duties (Evans 2013, 13).

A second concern about the Morality Framework derives from the evil-god challenge. This challenge claims that belief in an evil-god (i.e., a being that is omnipotent, omniscient, yet morally evil) is epistemically on par with belief in a morally good God. This challenge, if successful, plausibly weakens the prior probability of the Morality Framework, since the probability space would then minimally divide among three options (rather than one or two): a God who is morally perfect, morality-transcending, or evil.

Many responses to the evil-god challenge have been given (Symes 2024 presents a thorough discussion). One focuses on the intrinsic plausibility of the evil-god hypothesis. There is a long tradition of arguing that evil is parasitic on the good (see Anglin and Goetz 1982). If this is the case, an ontologically foundational wholly evil being is metaphysically impossible – a clear problem for the evil-god hypothesis. The hypothesis of a morally good God does not face this problem.

Another promising response is to argue for an epistemic asymmetry in the case of the good-God and evil-god hypotheses (see Layman 2022, 85–87; Hendricks 2023b). Whether or not an evil-god exists, belief in such a being is probably unjustified. This is because it is bad to hold unjustified beliefs, and an evil god would be motivated to bring about bad states of affairs. So an evil god would have reason to ensure that the beliefs of creatures about his existence are unjustified. By contrast, belief in a good God is probably justified if such a God exists. This can be supported by the kind of reasoning that undergirds arguments from divine hiddenness – knowing that God exists is a necessary condition for human well-being, so a morally good God would provide justification for belief in His existence. The relevant justified theistic belief may be understood as properly basic or as supported by evidence provided by God. If belief in an evil-god is unjustified whether or not an evil god exists, but this is not the case for belief in a good-God, then the latter hypothesis is more reasonable than the former.

Notice too that this epistemic response to the evil-god challenge gives the Morality Framework a comparative advantage on this score over the Holiness Framework. For the reasons noted, a God whose motives perfectly conform to moral norms can be expected to provide justified beliefs in Him. However, this is something that is not similarly expected on the Holiness Framework since, according to it, God has requiring reasons not to get intimately acquainted with creatures. As seen in Section 3, such reasons are what render divine hiddenness unsurprising. There consequently appears to be an epistemic asymmetry that favors the Morality Framework over the Holiness Framework.

Perhaps the strongest argument against the Morality Framework comes from Mark Murphy. As discussed in Section 3, Murphy (e.g., 2017, 45–66; 2021, 79–98) has developed a sophisticated argument against the Morality Framework based upon the logical gap between *some action's advancing or protecting someone else's welfare* and *one's having requiring reason to perform that action which advances or protects that person's welfare*. For the reasons expressed in Section 3, we maintain that the force of Murphy's argument, though impressive, is outweighed by other considerations. Such a case is strengthened in light of the epistemic considerations within the immediately preceding paragraph. Those who share this judgment may conclude that the case for the prior probability of the Morality Framework is reasonably (comparatively) high.

The Explanatory Power of the Morality Framework

The explanatory power of the Morality Framework may also be judged to be reasonably high. First, a significant segment of the Christian tradition has viewed God as a morally good being, plausibly a morally perfect being (see, e.g., Leftow 1989, 240). We see this in Clement of Alexandria (*Miscellanies*, 7.16.102) when he appeals to God's parental goodness to shed light on God's remedial punishment. We also find this in Origen of Alexandria's defense against the Gnostics on both biblical and philosophical grounds that God enjoys the virtues of justice and goodness, where moral evil is opposed to both (*De Principiis*, Book II, ch. 5). Likewise, we take St. Athanasius to be presupposing that God is merciful in morally recognizable ways when he claims that it would be "unworthy of God's goodness" to leave humans without hope of salvation

(1954, 1.6, p. 61). Even St. Thomas Aquinas possibly views God as a moral being (Echavarría 2022), despite the fact that some have expressly upheld Aquinas as maintaining that God transcends morality (e.g., Davies 2006, 2011; Murphy 2021, 97–98). In any case, later Protestant theologians certainly viewed God as morally perfect (see Williams 2021), albeit often not subject to many obligations impinging upon human behavior. As the Puritan theologian Stephen Charnock puts it, divine goodness "is that perfection of God whereby he delights in his works, and is beneficial to them [his creatures]. God is the highest goodness, because he doth not act for his own profit, but for his creatures' welfare" (1979, 219). Thus, appeals to the Christian tradition, or segments thereof, provide grounds to affirm that God is morally perfect.

Second, many biblical passages ostensibly describe God as morally good. Throughout the Psalms we find praise of God along the following lines: "You are good and do good" (Ps. 119:68; cf. 25:8; 86:5; 100:5; 146:7). Additionally, the Bible describes God as faithful and just (e.g., Deut. 32:4; 2 Thess. 1:6-8; 1 John 1:9) as well as loving, gracious, and compassionate (e.g., Exod. 34:6-7; Ps. 103:8; Joel 2:13; James 5:11; 1 John 4:7-21). Plausibly, the best explanation of such descriptions of God is that various biblical authors teach, or at least assume, that God is morally good (Leftow 2013, 69–70).

Additionally, many biblical passages enjoin people to trust in God (Ps. 62:8; Prov. 3:5; Isa. 26:4). But if God is not perfectly morally good, how would this trust be justified? Confidence that God will act morally grounds trust in Him.

Even biblical passages where people question God seem to indicate that the authors recognize that God ought to act according to moral standards. For example, Abraham reasons with God in Genesis 18: "Shall not the judge of all the earth do what is just?" Many biblical figures struggle with the question of "Why does the way of the wicked prosper?" (Jer. 12:1-2; cf., Job 21:7; Psalm 73:3) in light of God's providential oversight. But this is only a puzzle if one thinks that God is perfectly moral, and so ought to direct events morally.

Moreover, various biblical authors implore humans to behave in holy and loving ways because God is holy and loving (e.g., Lev. 11:44; Matt. 5:43-48; Jn. 15:9-12; Eph. 5:1-2; Phil. 2:1-8; 1 Pet. 1:13-15; Jn. 4:7-11). The idea is plausibly that the morality humans are to obey finds its origin in the moral God. There is also some biblical reason to suppose that God is not merely moral but also morally perfect. For example, at the climax of his exposition of a demanding ethic of love in his Sermon on the Mount, Jesus commands his followers to be "perfect" as their "heavenly Father is perfect" (Matt. 5:48). In the context, it is difficult to resist the sense that this imitable perfection refers to *moral* perfection (again, see, Leftow 2013, 70). Plus, once we grant that God is morally very good, it is simpler to maintain that God is morally perfect rather than merely morally good to some lesser degree (see Swinburne 2004, 97–98). Thus, there is at least a prima facie case to be made that Scripture supports the idea that God is morally good, and together with some adjunct assumptions, morally perfect.

The Morality Framework also naturally explains central aspects of Scripture's creation, redemption, and consummation arc. Why does God create, redeem, and glorify humans and creation more generally? Because these are morally good things to do, although more precise analyses of why a morally perfect God would do these things will depend upon the version of the Morality Framework affirmed. Similarly, God may be counted upon to punish the wicked and (occasionally) answer prayers because He is motivated to act morally.

Of course, some read Scripture differently (e.g., Lewis 1983 and Davies 2006). While Scripture plausibly teaches that human morality reflects the divine character in some way, that is not equivalent to the teaching that God acts in conformity to familiar moral norms. Establishing the latter thesis from Scripture is a more difficult task. Furthermore, Brian Davies contends that Scripture depicts God as an individual who does what He wills and does not need "to justify himself in the light of moral canons to which he is [. . .] obliged" (Davies 2006, 96).

Our view, however, is that Scripture provides strong evidence for the idea that God is a moral being, as overviewed. Put simply, the notion that Scripture does not support the claim that God is a moral being, in a mostly recognizable sense, would demand a fairly comprehensive reframing of how God is ubiquitously and straightforwardly described in Scripture (challenging depictions of God notwithstanding). If this is right, then a high burden of proof is placed upon the objector who accords Scripture a great deal of authority.

Nevertheless, there is one final issue to mention concerning the evaluation of the Morality Framework. There are many arguments from creaturely suffering (arguments from evil) or from apparent nonresistant nonbelief in God (arguments from divine hiddenness) to the conclusion that a morally perfect God does not exist. These arguments are typically given against God's existence. But one could utilize such arguments to support the comparative advantage of conceptions of God as transcending familiar morality over conceptions of God as perfectly moral (see Davies 2006 and Murphy 2017). In our view, this is a serious comparative issue that advocates of the Morality Framework must address. For even if various defenses, theodicies, and/or forms of skeptical theism succeed, it still may be that the Morality Framework is less probable than frameworks that affirm God as transcending familiar morality, given the former's inability to explain the problems of evil and divine hiddenness as well as these rivals.

Summary and Conclusion

There is a prima facie case to be made that the Morality Framework has a reasonably high prior probability and enjoys considerable explanatory power. Upon further examination, moreover, we found no considerations that would serve to diminish significantly the prior probability of the Morality Framework, unless one is taken by Murphy's argument from the existing gap between the goodness of well-being and requiring reason to promote/protect it. Nor have we located considerations that substantially reduce the explanatory power of the framework, with the possible exception that the Morality Framework does not fare as well as competing frameworks where God is thought to be morality-transcending in explaining evil and divine hiddenness. This issue will be discussed later. The noted caveats aside, our intermediate verdict is that the Morality Framework provides a plausible way of addressing the problem of divine motivation.

Why not hold to the Morality Framework, then? The fuller answer to this question will come into focus near the end of this Element, where we discuss the possibility that the Agapist Framework is a version of the Morality Framework. Still, one misgiving about the Morality Framework is worth presenting here. The bare Morality Framework does not give us sufficient insight into the structure of divine motivation. Suppose we agree that God's fundamental motivations perfectly conform to norms affiliated with perfect virtue and the satisfaction of obligations. The obvious follow-up question would be, Which virtues does God possess and which obligations does God have? It would be preferable to have an account of God's motivational structure that sheds greater light on the divine character and what God is inclined to do. The Agapist Framework we defend in the following sections intends to do just that.

5 The Agapist Framework

Christians understand God to be perfectly loving. Love eternally exists among the persons of the Trinity, and this primordial love is often thought to motivate why God creates, identities with creatures through the Incarnation, and dies a criminal's death to redeem sinful humans so that they might be forever united to Him in beatitude. Such a vision of God naturally lends itself to a kind of Love Framework, according to which God's love for humans constitutes the fundamental motive for God's dealings with these creatures. While there are several ways in which the Love Framework might be unpacked (see Oord 2015 and Schellenberg 2015 for two alternatives), this section focuses on explaining the version of the Love Framework that we find most plausible. We dub this version the Agapist Framework. We select this label for expediency and are not assuming a hard line between agape and eros as is sometimes done, or additional common affiliations with the term left unstated.

What Is Love?

Proponents of the Love Framework maintain that divine love holds the key to understanding God's fundamental motives concerning creation. However, to grasp the Love Framework, especially in its Agapist version, we need an account or model of divine love (see Wood 2016 and Crisp 2021 for the character and function of theological models). When it comes to modeling God's moral goodness, it is often assumed that God and humans are similar such that conceptions of divine goodness can be reasonably modeled after conceptions of human goodness (Garcia 2009, 221). Models of divine love are understood to be similar in this respect, and several such models have been proposed (see Wessling 2021 for an overview).

We cannot here enter a detailed debate about how best to model God's love. What is needed, then, is a generally agreeable way of understanding human love which serves, for present purposes, as a basis for a sufficiently precise model of divine love. Consider Gabriele Taylor's widely referenced description of human love:

> If x loves y then x wants to benefit and be with y etc., and he has these wants (or at least some of them) because he believes y has some determinate characteristics ψ in virtue of which he thinks it worthwhile to benefit and be with y. He regards satisfaction of these wants as an end and not as a means towards some other end. (Taylor 1975–1976, 157; similarly, Pruss 2012, 23)

Notice that Taylor's description captures three features or attitudes of love: benevolence (x wants to benefit y) and some kind of desire for union (x wants to be with y), both of which are had because there is a kind of attraction to the one loved or some kind of valuing of her (x has these wants because x believes that y's ψ warrant benefiting and being with y). Recent accounts of divine love tend to focus on one or two of these features (e.g., Hill 1984; Oord 2010, 19–30; and Stump 2010, 85–107). However, we think it best to include all three. So, a model of divine love that takes cues from Taylor may be understood as follows: God's love, when directed at a person, is that which responds to that individual's intrinsic worth by valuing both the existence and flourishing of that individual and a kind of union or interpersonal relationship with this individual. To value these states of affairs (i.e., the existence, flourishing, and union with this individual) is to represent them as good, as something to be pursued, promoted, preserved, embraced, or delighted in (see Oddie 2005). Call this the *value account* of divine love. Such a view has been clarified and defended at length elsewhere (Wessling 2020a), and we rely on this baseline model of divine love for the remainder of this section.

The Character of the Agapist Framework

Since God is maximally perfect, it is sensible to conclude that proponents of the Agapist Framework should say that God is fundamentally motivated by *perfect* love. However, this raises the question, How might perfect divine love be understood?

One way of understanding the perfection of divine love can be called *the ultimate degree view* (see Frankfurt 2009, 62–63; Murphy 2017, 34–42; Rea 2018, 63–89). Based on the idea that God's love can never be eclipsed in value, the proponent of the ultimate degree view submits that God's love is absolutely unsurpassable in terms of its depth and scope (minimally, for all existing entities): God must love every lovable being (maximal scope), and, for each being that God loves, God must love that being to a degree that could not possibly be exceeded (maximal depth). Were God to love some legitimately lovable being more than He loves another, or were God not to love some genuinely lovable being, then God would fail to exemplify love to the ultimate degree, and hence, *ex hypothesi*, would fail to qualify as a perfectly loving being.

Many have argued against the ultimate degree view. For instance, Jeff Jordan (e.g., 2015; 2020) argues that God loves some creature maximally only if God identifies with that creature's interests, that is, takes that creature's interests as His own. Yet, since creaturely interests often conflict, God simply cannot identify with the interests of creatures equally, and thus love them equally. To deny this, thinks Jordan, would require us to deny that God has a kind of intimate, partial love that is befitting of divine perfection (for critiques of Jordan's argument, see Parker 2013; Talbott 2020).

Coming from a different angle, Michael Rea (2018, 63–89) argues that something like the ultimate degree view entails that God is maximally devoted to the good of each human. But such maximal divine devotion would absurdly preclude God from having interests and concerns that are essential to having a personality. Rea furthermore maintains that mitigated divine devotion to creatures is a good thing. It is doubtful that we could bear the full force of God's limitless love. Such love is reserved for within the Trinity alone (2018, 78).

Finally, Mark Murphy (2017, 34–38) argues that it seems wrong to attribute what we are here calling the ultimate degree view to God. We commonly suppose that the degree to which one loves someone or something should correspond to the object of affection's level of worth. Because creatures possess differential worth, differential degrees of love seem most fitting. It is additionally doubtful that it makes sense to love some creature unsurpassably. There does not appear to be an upper limit to the well-being or level of union with Himself that God could will a creature.

We agree with Murphy that it's counterintuitive to suppose that God's love would not track with the "intrinsic" value of the entities loved. Given the differential worth, it seems mistaken to suppose that God should love blades of grass, sea anemones, cats, and humans equally and as much as He loves Himself, the absolutely greatest possible being.

Here is a sketch of a way of thinking about the matter. Suppose we identify God with The Good and agree that The Good is that which is worthy of admiration or love (Adams 1999, 13). Suppose also that all creatures only enjoy various limited forms of goodness, which, in one way or another, find their source in God as The Good. If The Good is that which is worthy of admiration or love, then it would seem that God, as The Good, would merit a higher degree of love than that which is only limited in goodness. By extension, it would also seem that various beings of limited goodness would, ceteris paribus, merit varying lower degrees or qualities of love. In that case, the ultimate degree view is false.

A more plausible alternative to the ultimate degree view is that God's maximally perfect love entails that God loves every lovable being to the *optimal level* (see Murphy 2017, 42–43, for a slightly different use of the term). The proponent of the optimal level view maintains that God's maximal love should be cashed out by way of the best and highest *fit* between the divine affection and value of the object beloved. The higher the intrinsic value of the beloved, the greater the quality or degree of merited love.

The optimal level view requires that there is an objective standard according to which beings should be loved. At the lower end, to fail to love some individual at some minimal level reveals a deficient love. At the upper end, to love some being beyond an upper bound would be to love that being too much or perversely, or perhaps to venture into territory that is not true love at all. The optimal level view provides an account of God's maximal love insofar as its proponents maintain that God necessarily loves individuals at the highest level of objective fittingness – that is, at, but not beyond, the relevant upper bound, which constitutes the most valuable form of fitting love relative to the being at issue. Qualifications to the optimal level view will be discussed subsequently. But given certain value commitments, the optimal level view entails that God loves Himself to an unsurpassable degree, and He loves creatures differentially to the highest level that their various degrees of intrinsic value afford.

The idea that there is this relevant objective fit strikes us as reasonable (*pace* Nygren 1982, which is critiqued in Wessling 2020a, 73–74). Start with the idea that there is an objective upper bound to the strength of divine love. Rea (2018, 78–79) contends that unfettered divine devotion to a human entails the absurd conclusion that God worships this human. Thus, insofar as we maintain that ever increasing depths of love eventually become forms of worship, there must be some upper bound to God's love of creatures, even if we cannot specify this limit. Additionally, many have the sense that it would be untoward that God unqualifiedly loves a human with the level of love that exists within the Trinity.

Intuitively, moreover, there is an upper bound to the type and degree of love that God ought to direct toward various types of creatures. It seems, for instance, that there would be something mismatched about God loving mushrooms or cockroaches as much as He does humans. It is not that mushrooms and cockroaches are unworthy of any type of love, but they don't seem to be good candidates for the kind or depth of love that God lavishes on humans. Different kinds of creatures have different upper bounds.

It similarly seems that certain creatures enjoy an objective lower bound on how they ought to be loved. Two conditions factor into setting this lower bound for God's love of humans (see Wessling 2020a, 164–165). The first condition is that humans are tremendously valuable. Indeed, if one holds that humans enjoy dignity, they may be said to be equal in value *qua* human or as persons. While there are numerous accounts of this tremendous value, the thinking behind this first condition is that high degrees of intrinsic worth warrant (sometimes even demand) a particular love-response, and the higher the degree of value, the greater the response merited. This is arguably why it makes sense for Christians to teach that God should be loved above all else and worshiped, and why, ceteris paribus, humans should love other humans more than dogs.

The second condition has to do with the idea that God created humans in need of a certain baseline level of love. God has made us for Himself, St. Augustine reminds us; consequently, our hearts are restless until they find rest in Him (*Confessions* 1.1). Expanding upon Augustine's insight, if we were made for a loving relationship with God, then it seems that it would be untoward, perhaps even cruel, to make us in this manner and yet not love us to the degree that is necessary to fulfill our created purposes. Worse than that, on the Christian scheme, if humans are not loved by God to a degree in which God seeks their highest good, hell is inevitable. According to the Christian faith, therefore, humans radically depend upon the love of God. Our contention is these two conditions together indicate that there is some baseline level at which humans should be loved by God.

So far, then, it seems reasonable that there is the relevant kind of objective fit between creatures and the love of God. Nevertheless, there remains the challenge of spelling out what it means for God to love some individual at the optimal level or strength. Such a strength of love might be cashed out in terms of intensity of feeling, the benefits chosen for the one loved, dispositions to act, and so on. Hence, there are numerous options that the defender of the Agapist Framework might pursue. We find it most fruitful to think of the strength of God's love in terms of the weight of God's reasons for action and God's response to them. Generally, the intrinsically weightier the reasons are in God's deliberative processes, the stronger the love.

To grasp how this might go, recall that for God to love some human, Smith, is for God to respond to Smith's worth by valuing Smith's existence and flourishing and union with Smith. To value these states of affairs centered on Smith is to represent them as good; it is a way of responding to Smith's worth by affirming the noted states of affairs regarding Smith. Such a form of valuing is correlated with both *teleological* and *expressive* reasons for action. The former refers to having reasons to bring about or perpetuate states of affairs. In the context of God's love, examples include reasons to promote and preserve Smith's flourishing and union with Smith. Expressive reasons, which are perhaps more fundamental, are those that involve expressing, acknowledging, or respecting Smith's worth (see Anderson 1995; Scanlon 1998, 78–107; Murphy 2021, 120–125). Context often determines how these expressive attitudes relate to reasons for action, but examples of such reasons include reasons to attend to, delight in, or symbolically identify with Smith's worth and flourishing and to avoid situations and conditions in which Smith's worth is demeaned. Both teleological and expressive reasons for action might be understood to be generated by love's valuing or to exist prior to such valuing, or some combination thereof. We find it most plausible to maintain that, at least in most circumstances, love's valuing is acutely sensitive to and inclined to act upon antecedently existing reasons.

In keeping with the value account, God's reasons of love are explained by value or goodness. Generally, the weight of God's reasons of love corresponds to the intrinsic value of the being loved and to the value related to that being's flourishing and union with that being; the higher the value of the relevant being and the states of affairs related to her flourishing and union with her, the weightier God's teleological and expressive reasons are. The proponent of the optimal level view of divine love should maintain that these teleological and expressive reasons of love are typically intrinsically weightier than other reasons God has concerning creation, and that when they are such, they are decisive for God. In other words, God is perfectly inclined to act in conformity to the weight of His reasons, and the noted kinds of reasons of love typically outweigh other creation-related reasons God might have to act.

To put meat on these bones, let's focus on the teleological reasons of divine love to advance human flourishing and divine-human union. Here there are two broad options.

First, there is the *strong optimal level view*. Since God loves each human optimally, God has, for every human, *requiring* reason to bring about the highest available flourishing and divine-human union in each relevant circumstance. Since such requiring reasons are typically unopposed, such love-related reasons are regularly decisive for God. Stated differently, for every human that exists, God does whatever He feasibly (or acting in accordance with perfect practical rationality) can to promote and protect the highest form of human flourishing and divine-human union; such promotion and protection is generally God's highest priority in His dealings with humans. God does this as an expression of the highest fitting strength of His (strong) optimal love.

However, this optimal level view faces a challenge (à la Murphy 2017, 42–43). For any level of human flourishing or divine-human union that God could will, it seems God could always will more. But there plausibly needs to be an intrinsic maximum to such things if there is to be a highest objective fit by which God can love a human, in keeping with the strong optimal level view of divine love.

The defender of the strong optimal level view has many responses to this challenge. Consider the following options.

First, one might think there *is* an intrinsic maximum to the flourishing and the union that God can will for a human. It might be that what is good for a human is defined by the development or fulfillment of her human nature, and that human nature has built-in limitations to the amount of good that God can will for an individual. Similarly, it might be that the quality of union between God and humans is constrained by the limits of human nature, such that God is unable to will ever-increasing depths of divine-human union.

Suppose, though, that there is no greatest level of flourishing and union with God for humans. Their flourishing and union with God could always be improved. Still, God could will the best process, or life-trajectory, for humans. God can will *epektatic* union with humans: an everlasting condition of ever-increasing unity with God (see Gregory of Nyssa, *The Life of Moses*, 1.5-10). Perhaps our present earthly struggles are integral to shaping us for this process and so cannot be pointed to as reason to suppose that God has not given us the very best process.

Even if *epektasis* is the highest kind of good God could give any creature, one might wonder if there is not more God could do for humanity. Suppose, for instance, that Homer loves donuts. God could then give Homer *epektatic* communion with Himself *and* a half-dozen donuts each day. In such a case, Homer would have his highest singular good with a bit of extra on the side. The combination of these two goods seems to be better than *epektasis* alone, and since there is no obvious limit to such combinations of goods, it looks as if there is no highest total good God could give to any human. Hence, it appears that we do not have the highest intrinsic maximum we seek.

The defender of the strong optimal level view might respond by appealing to incommensurability and non-additivity. Perhaps the *epektatic* communion *trumps* the donuts or any creaturely goods in something like James Griffin's sense concerning incommensurability (1986, 83): *epektatic* communion with God is more valuable for Homer than any amount of donuts or other combined creaturely goods are for Homer. Furthermore, *epektasis* plus available donuts cannot be added together to produce a total value that is greater for Homer than the *epektatic* communion alone. The latter view makes sense given the idea that all the world's goodness is exemplified by the God to which the human is *epektatically* united. While these value claims are controversial and can be explicated in several ways, the root idea is that we can plausibly deny that God's providing a human *epektatic* union plus donuts (and a pet tiger, and a personal amusement park, etc.) manifests greater love than the *epektatic* union alone.

It might be helpful to think about the immediately preceding viewpoint from a different angle. Theists generally agree that God was entirely fulfilled prior to His creative act; God possessed all the resources for His own happiness within His own being. Yet when God creates, there is a sense in which God gains certain goods. Does this increase the quality of God's happiness or what is good for God? Most theists will answer "No!" While God might undergo an extensive increase in happiness – an increase in the scope and kinds of entities from which God derives happiness – the increase is not intensive – that is, deeper or richer in value or quality of experience. Similarly, although giving Homer donuts daily might provide an extensive increase in Homer's happiness, it does not provide an intensive one. If this is right, the defender of the optimal level view can maintain that the intrinsic maximum of human flourishing sought by divine love concerns the *epektatic* union which cannot be improved upon intensively.

Not everyone will be convinced by this way of specifying the relevant intrinsic maximum in favor of the strong optimal level view. An objector might reason that there are clear cases where goods alongside *epektatic* union advance the flourishing of humans. Although giving Homer daily donuts does not appear to increase Homer's flourishing intensively, reuniting Homer with his beloved childhood dog, Bongo, would make the relevant addition. For Bongo helped shape Homer's lasting character and was deeply loved by

Homer. Returning Bongo to Homer would add to Homer's overall life story in a meaningful manner. More generally, the redemptive reintegration of earthly goods back into Homer's life would seem to increase the quality of Homer's flourishing in a way in which arbitrary creaturely goods, such as donuts, would not.

Notice, though, that there is a finite number of meaningful earthly goods that can be reintegrated into Homer's heavenly bliss. Homer only had so many experiences before his pre-resurrection life came to an end. But if there is only a finite number of the relevant meaningful earthly goods, then it appears that God can reintegrate all the goods for which it is possible to do so (see Stump 2010, 369–481). If it is possible to resurrect a dog, then we might suppose that God will resurrect Bongo for Homer. If it would be possible for Homer to be reunited with his beloved child Lisa, then perhaps God would do that too (although human freedom plausibly limits the possibilities available to God). The point is that it is likely that there are only so many earthly goods that can be reintegrated into Homer's life to maximize his flourishing. Hence, it's unclear that the addition of certain other goods alongside *epektatic* union precludes an intrinsic maximum to human happiness which can be sought by the God who loves humans optimally.

A final way of specifying the relevant intrinsic maximum sought by divine love is to propose that God gives humans two kinds of ever-evolving goods. The first is *epektatic* union with Himself, and the second is an ever-increasing amount of post-mortem creaturely goods. If God can always add to the level of human flourishing by providing creaturely goods alongside *epektatic* union with Himself, God would give more and more goods for all eternity. Assuming there is an upper bound on *the rate* at which humans can receive and appreciate creaturely goods, then God gives humans the very best process (or one among the very best available processes) since there is no best singular or collective good to give humans.

The second way to understand reasons of divine love is the *weak optimal level view*. Recall from Section 3 the structure for divine action defended by Chris Tucker (2020). Tucker contends that God has requiring reasons to ensure that human lives are fully good (including, we add, lives sufficiently related to Him) but only justifying reasons to ensure that these lives are any degree better than this minimum threshold. The proponent of the weak optimal level view adopts this conception of God's reasons. God loves each human optimally in that He has requiring reasons, which are typically intrinsically weightier than other human-concerning reasons, to promote each human's fully good life. To strengthen the view, it might be said that since God is fundamentally motivated by love, God does whatever He feasibly (or practically rationally) can do to secure a fully good life for each human; this is generally God's chief priority in His dealings with humans. Unless God has sufficiently weighty countervailing reasons, God has decisive reason to ensure the instantiation of, or the path to, a fully good life for each human in each relevant circumstance. In this way, God loves each human (weakly) optimally. Of course, since God has justifying reasons to go beyond aiming at fully good lives, He may rationally choose to do so (when countervailing reasons do not preclude it) on the weak optimal level view. But this is not what the view requires of divine love.

One worry about the weak optimal level view is that it is too lenient. The advocate of the Agapist Framework emphasizes that God's maximal love has implications for God's motives concerning creation, and since it seems untoward to suppose that God loves humans and other creatures unsurpassably, the notion of optimality is brought in. God is said to love each creature at the *highest* most fitting level, as an expression of God's maximally loving but perfectly discerning nature. Yet the defender of the weak optimal level view (unlike the stronger variety) says that God's love does not require giving humans the available best, since God would be justified in giving humans better lives. So, such a view does not seem to be truly optimal.

The defender of the weak optimal level view might respond that this objection is based on an excessive focus on outcomes. It is better to maintain that God loves optimally by responding to His available reasons fittingly. Within each circumstance, God loves each human optimally by appreciating each human's value and appropriately weighing the reasons affiliated with that value (reasons that are intrinsically significant for God). Such a view pairs particularly well with the value account of divine love, where expressive reasons are more foundational than teleological reasons. For, on the value account, God responds to each human's worth by valuing (or representing as good) her existence, flourishing, and union with her. Valuing these states of affairs concerning the human loved is more naturally parsed in terms of expressive rather than teleological reasons, although the former will often cause or otherwise facilitate the latter (see Wessling 2020a, 51). If what is essential to divine love is perfect conformity to the right expressive reasons, and only derivatively about responding appropriately to the right teleological reasons, then the weak optimal level view seems sensible (compare with Leftow 2019, 304–305). God loves each human at the highest level of objective fittingness by having the relevant weighty expressive reasons, and the teleological reasons derived therefrom, and perfectly conforming to them.

It is worth mentioning that given certain axiological commitments, the weak and strong optimal level views might not be worlds apart. For instance, if it can be shown that there is a maximum to human flourishing and union with God, or that *epektatic* union with God is the best process for God to select, then this may incline proponents of the weak optimal level view to join advocates of the strong optimal level view in affirming that God has requiring reasons to select these options. As noted in Section 3, qualitative differences in the axiological landscape intuitively ought to match differences in the kinds of reasons God has. Nevertheless, proponents of the weak optimal level view aren't committed to there being the relevant kinds of differences in the axiological landscape.

Whether one favors the stronger or weak optimal level view, we submit that it is reasonable to maintain that God loves all beings optimally. When it comes to various existing creatures, God loves them with the highest quality and strength that befits their level of worth. Proponents of the Agapist Framework maintain that God's optimal love comprises God's fundamental motive for His engagement with humans, understood in accordance with either the weak or strong optimal level view.

Clearly, the Agapist Framework has been articulated in a manner that presupposes a broadly rationalist or intellectualist conception of divine motivation. God's love responds perfectly to the relevant objective reasons. Some deny this picture, though, opting instead for an account where God has brute preferences alongside objective reasons for action. Hence, God's love for beings is not always entirely explained by the antecedent and objective weight of the reasons God has for such love (e.g., Leftow 2017; Draper 2019; Wilson 2022).

One rationale for favoring the brute preference position of divine motivation is as follows (Leftow 2017, 156–158). Consider a circumstance where God has a choice between only equal or incommensurate options. If the pure rationalist perspective is right, then God cannot choose one of these options based on its reasons, since such reasons do not favor one choice over the other. In that sense, the choice would need to be arbitrary. However, if God has nonrational preferences, God may select an option for its features that are attractive to God. Being responsive to the selected option's features seems to be more rational than simply picking arbitrarily.

However, two considerations count against this argument. First, it apparently overlooks that rational agents not only have first-order reasons to select some option but second-order as well: reasons to act, or not, for some reason (Raz 1999, 39). If two options are totally equal, God evinces expected practical rationality (*pace* Leftow 2017, 155) when He opts for a second-order reason simply to pick one of the two available equally good options. Second, even on the brute preference view, it is possible that God could face choices between two equally good objective options about which God has no preference. In such cases, God would need to rely upon something like second-order reasons to make rational choices. The brute preference model thereby offers no advantages in this respect.

Another purported benefit of the brute preference model is that it enables us to say that God has His own personality (Wilson 2022, 76; cf. Rea 2018, 74–75). God, in other words, has unique preferences that sometimes guide His actions; He doesn't simply tally the available reasons and slavishly follow their dictates.

But why think that having a personality requires brute preferences? If it does, it seems to be at most a requirement for *creatures* who are subject to constraints and causal conditions outside their control. It may be that God's personality is simply "too big" for brute idiosyncrasies. His personality takes in all reality rather than being forced to delight idiosyncratically in certain features of it.

We should also consider God's sovereignty here. Many theists maintain that everything that exists is explained either by the necessity of the divine nature or by the will (or permission) of God. But God just finding Himself with preferences for certain creaturely goods either violates this constraint or postulates the apparently odd view that God necessarily yet arbitrarily favors some goods over others. Our preference is to avoid either option by rejecting the brute preference view.

A final stated advantage of the brute preferences model is that it enables God to create humans out of love rather than to maximize value. This is because "Love is a paradigm nonrational influence; the rationalist picture [of divine motivation] leaves no room for it" (Leftow 2017, 165). It is controversial, though, that love is a nonrational influence (even if nonrational factors are involved) when ideally exemplified, even in the human case (see Hichem 2022). Indeed, we doubt the claim and have provided the foregoing Agapist Framework to the contrary. Additionally, if one opts for the weak optimal level view, one need not hold that rationalistic forms of love incline God toward an unqualified maximization of values.

We find the rationalist picture of divine motivation more attractive than the alternative. Behind the rationalistic picture rests the noted consideration pertaining to divine sovereignty. Similarly, theists want to deny that God is ever inappropriately made to act one way over another, either by external (and perhaps contingent) constraints or by internal drives and influences that are not themselves subject to rational assessment or the divine will. One way of meeting these desiderata is via the rationalist picture of divine motivation (see, Swinburne 2016, 142–149; Murphy 2017, 27). So, we utilize it for the Agapist Framework. The defender of the Agapist Framework who remains attracted to the brute preference picture of divine motivation should say that God's objective reasons and preferences related to love together comprise God's fundamental motives concerning humans. But we leave it to readers to consider how to conceive of the details of such a brute preference model.

6 The Plausibility of the Agapist Framework

Now that the basic contours of the Agapist Framework are before us, consider the framework's plausibility. As with the other frameworks evaluated, this consideration involves an assessment of the prior probability and explanatory power of the Agapist Framework.

The Prior Probability of the Agapist Framework

Two sources feed into the assessment of the prior probability of the Agapist Framework: the doctrine of the Trinity and the absolute perfection of the divine nature.

The doctrine of the Trinity is agreed upon by defenders of the various motivational frameworks considered in this Element. It's a teaching that Christians often *bring to* the assessment of some motivational framework's explanatory power. So we take the doctrine of the Trinity to factor into the assessment of the Agapist Framework's prior probability. We argue that the doctrine of the Trinity raises the prior probability of the Agapist Framework.

Christians emphasize intra-trinitarian love. The love here is maximal; it is impossible for there to be a more valuable kind of love than that which exists within the Trinity. While there might be virtues besides love that inform the intra-trinitarian life, love is thought to be central to the life of the triune God. Indeed, love is usually the primary attribute appealed to in a priori arguments for the Trinity (e.g., Swinburne 1994, ch. 8; Sijuwade 2024). Although such arguments remain controversial, their reliance on widely affirmed convictions about the depth of intra-trinitarian love is rarely the point of contention.

That love suffuses the triune life does not prove the Agapist Framework. But the more one emphasizes the triune God of love, the more expected the Agapist Framework becomes. After all, if some or all creatures resemble the divine nature that God loves, then this plausibly gives God compelling reason to love each creature which resembles God's nature. This is especially the case for those creatures who can return love to God and resemble, however faintly, the intra-trinitarian love. And when one loves another deeply (which God may well do in the case of humans), this normally corresponds with weighty reasons to act accordingly.

When God's love is understood along the lines of the (weak or strong) optimal level view described in Section 5, we should expect God's maximal intra-trinitarian love to inform His love of creatures, albeit appropriately calibrated to their level of worth. As a maximally loving being, in other words, God loves each existing being in the highest fitting way, since this is the most valuable manner of loving. Given that the doctrine of the Trinity reveals God as maximally loving, we conclude that the Agapist Framework enjoys a relatively high prior probability. Minimally, this framework does not suffer from a low prior probability compared to competing divine motivational frameworks.

Another way to argue for a comparatively high prior probability for the Agapist framework is by the method of perfect being theology. Simply stated, if love is a good characteristic to have (a pure perfection), then the maximally great being, God, will be perfect in love. And if God is perfect in love, God will love creatures, particularly rational creatures such as humans that can return God's love, optimally. Against this, someone might argue that perfect divine love is incompatible with other divine perfections and so cannot be attributed to God. But we doubt that there is any such incompatibility, and in Section 5 we attempted to give an account of optimal love that may be reasonably attributed to God. Thus, in our estimation, reflections related to perfect being theology raise the prior probability of the Agapist Framework.

The Explanatory Power of the Agapist Framework

The explanatory power of the Agapist Framework can be assessed along various biblical, theological, and philosophical dimensions. We highlight some of the most important considerations.

First, the Agapist Framework has excellent explanatory power concerning the great themes of Scripture (see Rutledge and Wessling 2023). Consider, for instance, the biblical emphasis on a God that covenants with people and wants them to know Him and how they should live. One plausible explanation of these actions is that God cares about humans and wants them to flourish in relationships with Him. Such divine concern is precisely what we should expect if the Agapist Framework is true.

The Agapist Framework also explains creation well. As Ian McFarland (2014, 57) asserts, "God is love" and "the inherent productivity of this love makes it natural that it should expand beyond the bounds of God's own being." Approached from a different angle, the Agapist Framework provides a natural way of understanding the Dionysian Principle that the good is diffusive of itself (Kretzmann 1991, 217). Because divine love is an appreciative response to values, which is accompanied by teleological reasons for action (see Section 5), God has reason to create beings that He recognizes as having value should He choose to actualize them (see Wessling 2020a, 107–111).

What is more, biblical scholars argue that Scripture depicts God as fashioning creation as a kind of cosmic temple so that He might indwell it (e.g., Beale 2014; Middleton 2014). Obviously, this is a deeply intimate way of relating to creation that surpasses mere omnipresence. We suggest that such a unitive purpose for creation is predicted well by the Agapist Framework.

A criticism of the Agapist Framework is that it explains creation too well, leading to a necessitarianism about creation (Murphy 2021, 137–145). But, should this necessitarianism prove problematic, defenders of the Agapist Framework might point to plausible reasons that God has not to create, thereby rendering creation contingent (see Rutledge and Wessling 2023, 449–450). Another option might be to propose that God has only justifying reason, not requiring reason, to create, thereby implying the contingency of creation. To create, after all, seems to be an act of grace; nonexistent beings have no claim on God's actions. Prior to creation there are no creatures to love. (Hence proponents of the Agapist Framework should say that God creates *for the sake of* love, not *out of* love; see Wessling 2020a, 109–110). However, once the creatures exist, the requirements of love change. Having created humans, God then has requiring reasons in keeping with the optimal level view of divine love.

The Agapist Framework also explains God's incarnation and the great lengths God went to procure human salvation. Such salvation includes not just the forgiveness of sins, won by humiliating crucifixion, but also the Spirit's indwelling and (many think) the deification of humanity. These are profound acts of identification and humble love, acts that a God motivated fundamentally by self-glorification, justice, duty, or holiness is unlikely to perform.

There is another line of biblical support for the Agapist Framework that makes use of New Testament teaching about a foundational moral principle, namely, love. Consider, first, that Jesus and various New Testament authors teach that love fulfills the law (e.g., Matt. 22:34-40; Rom. 13:8-10; Gal. 5:14; Jas. 2:8). There is certainly debate about what love as the fulfillment of the law might mean (and there might be differences of understanding among the relevant biblical figures), but it may be reasonably supposed that it means that love *completes* human morality: loving each relevant individual in the most valuable feasible way determines, for any action (including mental actions), whether the action ought to be done or not (Howard-Snyder 2005, 3–4). So understood, loving in the ideal way fulfills (even while surpassing) the demands of the law. Second, Jesus, as well as certain biblical authors, ground this completed human ethic of love on God's nature (e.g., Matt. 5:43-48; Lk. 6:28-36; Jn. 13:31-35, 15:9-12; Eph. 5:1-2; 1 Jn. 4:7-21). That is to say, according to these texts, the love to which Christians are called reflects, or closely resembles,

God's character of love (see Borg 1998, 125–143). Taken together, these two biblical teachings (or the interpretations thereof) support the Agapist Framework. If humans are called to love in a manner that completes morality, and this completed morality closely resembles the character of God, then it stands to reason that there is no divine moral action or moral virtue (or that which is analogous thereto) that is not fundamentally a way of loving. If this is so, then it looks as if God's fundamental motives are in keeping with the Agapist Framework.

We may think about the matter as follows. Either God is subject to moral norms or He is not. If He is, then, for the reasons just stated, it looks as if God's most significant moral norms are those explained by, or are features of, love. But, as noted in Section 2, moral norms provide weighty reasons for action that cannot be blamelessly ignored without sufficient cause. By their very nature, moral norms tend to give the individual who is subject to them overriding reason to act in accordance with them. If this is so, and if God's moral norms fundamentally concern ways of loving, then God's fundamental motives will be expressions of love, in keeping with the Agapist Framework.

Suppose, though, that God is not subject to moral norms. God loves, but it would be a mistake to suppose that God is subject to norms of love that should be described as moral. Nonetheless, that the human ethic of love should reflect the divine nature according to the biblical texts previously cited suggests that love plays a role in the divine life that is analogous to a moral norm, the most significant moral norm at that. For example, Marcus Borg (1998, 137, cf. 139) is on the right track when he says, in commenting on Matthew 5:45, that "Jesus' ethic, in short, was based upon an *imitatio dei* [. . .]," that is, reflecting the loving divine character and imitating loving divine behavior. But it does not seem that Christians could resemble God's character well in their ethic (which is supposed to be principally about love) if love is not central to who God is and how He treats others. Once again, this is predicted well by the Agapist Framework.

William Lane Craig (2023, 3) objects to the idea that love's fulfillment of the law as a reflection of the divine character provides good grounds for supposing that God's most fundamental moral norm or virtue is love. The core of the critique is that Jesus's statement about love fulfilling the law concerns the positive demands of the law, not what must be done to those who break the law and hence deserve punishment.

Three lines of evidence indicate that Craig's critique fails. First, the division between fulfilling the positive demands of the law and what must be done to lawbreakers does not survive scrutiny. On the contrary, the Mosaic law which Jesus has in mind in passages such as Matthew 22:34-40 includes how lawbreakers should be punished (e.g., Ex 21:23-25; Lev 24:20; Deut 19:21).

Second, in Matthew 5:43-48, Jesus arguably maintains that his followers should love others in their punitive actions so that they might reflect the character of God who brings both sunlight and rain to even the evil and unrighteous (5:45; cf. Wessling 2020a, 200–206). It is in this way that they fulfill, even while surpassing, the demands of the law (compare Matt 5:48 with 5:17-20), and reflect the divine character. Third, Jesus's statement about love fulfilling the law in Matthew 22:37-40 quotes Leviticus 19:18b, where the Israelites are told to love their neighbors as themselves. Significantly, the love command in its Levitical context immediately follows the injunctive, "You shall not take vengeance or bear a grudge against any of your people" (Lev 19:18a). Issues related to just punishment also arise within surrounding verses in Leviticus 19 (19:5-8; 19:15-16; 19:20-22). So, it looks as if love of one's neighbor concerns punitive treatment, contrary to Craig's counter-argument. By contrast, the Agapist Framework predicts the (apparent) NT teaching that the love which reflects the divine character completes morality.

It's worth pausing to consider a respect in which the Agapist Framework appears superior to certain versions of the Morality Framework. Take the idea that God is fundamentally motivated by justice and that God's love plays a secondary role in God's motivational structure. On Jonathan Kvanvig's reading (1993, 117–118), Nicholas Malebranche affirmed such a view. More recently, William Lane Craig (2023) has articulated a similar position, where righteousness is the central divine moral attribute. However, as Kvanvig notes, this perspective has difficulty explaining creation. Justice/righteousness is a reactive attitude, not that which is creative. The emphasis on justice/righteousness is also difficult to square with God's gracious redemptive plan, which involves a humiliating form of identification with wayward humans. By contrast, as we have seen, both of these actions are explained well by the Agapist Framework.

Of course, emphasizing God's love brings with it the challenge of dealing with biblical depictions of divine wrath. Such wrath can come in the form of apparently indiscriminate killings, severe punishments, and damnation.

We start with apparently indiscriminate divine killings. In various passages, Israel is commanded to obliterate Canaanites, sparing neither young nor old nor noncombatants (e.g., Num 31:17-18; 1 Sam 15:3). These passages appear to paint a rather harsh picture of God's character – a picture that is prima facie difficult to square with the Agapist Framework. However, these passages serve as a comparative argument against the Agapist Framework only if the other frameworks under consideration fare better in explaining these passages. But this doesn't seem to be the case with every comparison. God's command to kill the Canaanites seems at least prima facie difficult to square with Glorificationism and the Morality Framework as well. These passages might also be problematic for the Holiness Framework if one acknowledges that the Holy God has requiring reasons not to intend evil for creatures (see Murphy 2021, 153). Further, Christians have developed methods of dealing with these passages that appear to be compatible with the Agapist Framework (for surveys of procedures, see Seibert 2016; Boyd 2017, 335–462; Rauser 2021). These methods include just war, error, allegory/spiritualization, hyperbole, and a redemptive or Christological hermeneutic, which may be combined in various ways. In light of these two considerations, these passages provide at most only modest comparative evidence against the Agapist Framework.

Turn, next, to the issue of severe divine punishments for individual wrongdoing. It may be thought that Scripture provides evidence against the Agapist Framework insofar as it depicts God punishing individuals in ways that are positively and irredeemably bad for them, even *if* such punishment is deserved (e.g., striking people dead or damning them). But again, Christians have given various accounts of how to reconcile divine punishment with divine love.

One option might be called the *natural consequences view* (Hanson 1957). According to it, God allows sinful humans to experience the awful yet eventually inevitable consequences of their own behavior. Generally, the natural penalty of a vicious life is becoming a vicious person, and the vicious person ultimately cannot flourish. It might be thought that this divine approach to dealing with human sin is not only biblically preferable to the severe punitive alternative but also befitting of God's love. It manifests a way in which God respects the choices of even His most wayward creatures. If the natural consequences view comprises a plausible reading of Scripture, then the challenge to the Agapist Framework seems to dissolve.

There is also the *retributive punishment view*, where divine punishment is given as the just desert for wrongdoing. Yet it can be argued that God loves the recipients of His punishment by treating them as responsible agents. In doing so, God acts in accordance with the good of those punished. This can be united with the idea that God only punishes humans in this way when He knows that they are morally hardened such that there is no hope for repentance.

Finally, there is a view which seeks to combine retributivist and remedial elements: *divine communicative punishment* (Wessling 2020b; 2022, 47–52; and 2023). On this perspective, God's punishment aims to communicate to offenders the censure they deserve (the retributivist component) with the purpose of providing a context in which these wrongdoers can wrestle with their offenses and, if willing, seek redemption (the remedial component). It may be that God administers communicative punishment through secondary agents (e.g., Romans 13:1–5) or in a more direct fashion (think of the final judgment).

God may also use various communicative strategies in punishment. God, for instance, might relevantly communicate diachronically by weaving together events or by highlighting things to which sinners should attend via the power of the Spirit. This can be fleshed out through postmortem opportunities for redemption (including in hell), or, for those who understand opportunities for redemption to be limited to this life, through God offering people a final opportunity for repentance in the process of dying. Regardless of the precise communicative means utilized, God's punitive wrath is at root an expression of God's love since it carries within it the potential for redemption.

There is certainly much that could be questioned on these matters about divine wrath. But if one of the canvassed theological proposals succeeds, or if they can be combined successfully, then it seems the Agapist Framework has considerable explanatory power without suffering from great amounts of anomalous data. Yet there remain two serious challenges to the Agapist Framework: the problems of evil and divine hiddenness. A detailed treatment of these issues obviously cannot be undertaken in this Element. Only a few general comments on behalf of the Agapist Framework can be provided. We consider theodicies, skeptical theism, and then a combination of the two.

While evil and divine hiddenness are prima facie surprising given the Agapist Framework, there are also ways in which these negative features of the world are plausibly predicted by this framework. For example, the Agapist Framework plausibly predicts moral evil since a loving God can be expected to give rational creatures libertarian free will, including the valuable ability to choose whether to return God's love to Him. But significant freedom of this kind comes with the possibility of incredible moral evil (Swinburne 1998; Boyd 2001; Manis 2016, 307–308). Some add that human autonomy sometimes would be inhibited improperly were God less hidden (e.g., Swinburne 1998; Murray 2002), and perhaps would preclude valuable forms of self-sacrificial love (Cullison 2010, 126–131). Similarly, the Agapist Framework plausibly predicts a range of struggles and obstacles, including divine hiddenness, in order for humans to have the opportunity to shape their characters through a history of moral choices. In forming their characters in this way, humans possess a measure of aseity that resembles God (see Irenaeus, *Against Heresies* 4.37.4). It is unsurprising that a loving God would provide humans with this opportunity to resemble the maximally great being. Additionally, it might be that God hides from some so that they come to Him with better motives and are disposed to be transformed more completely when they find Him (e.g., Howard-Snyder 1996; Moser 2008). Finally, the Agapist Framework raises the expectation that God would value deep and lasting interpersonal (loving) connections forged out of virtuous responses to evil, thus paving the way for the *connection-building theodicy* (Collins 2013). The claim is not that the Agapist Framework is the only framework that predicts these outcomes, but plausibly it predicts many of them better than alternative frameworks.

The Agapist Framework may also be compatible with skeptical theism, the position that we are unjustified in making all-things-considered judgments about what God would do or permit in any given situation. The two ideas can be plausibly thought to be compatible since one can become convinced of the Agapist Framework for considerations that do not obviously violate the strictures of skeptical theism. Such a violation does not obviously occur, for instance, when one concludes that the Agapist Framework makes the most sense of the intuition that love is a great-making property, that love is the triune God's most defining virtue, and that God reveals Himself as wondrously loving toward humans in Scripture's salvation arc, culminating in the person of Christ. Furthermore, once it is agreed that God is fundamentally motivated by love in His dealings with humans, this does not clearly entail that we are justified in supposing that God would never allow instances of great suffering, in keeping with skeptical theism. The Agapist Framework commits us to certain claims about the place of love in God's deliberative processes; it does not clearly commit us to any level of confidence about how God's reasons of love, working together with other kinds of reasons, dictate what kinds of evils God will allow in any given circumstance. If this is right, proponents of the Agapist Framework (as well as other frameworks) can use skeptical theism to defuse challenges from both evil and divine hiddenness to their preferred paradigm.

However, the use of skeptical theism raises a worry. If we cannot make the relevant all-things-considered judgments, one wonders if the Agapist Framework has much predictive power. If it does not, one might question the value of the Agapist Framework and also worry that it cannot be confirmed in the manner indicated in this section.

Consider the following way of responding to this worry (greatly inspired by Hendricks 2023a, ch. 8). Skeptical theism questions inferences from the *perceived* weight of God's reasons or the value of some state of affairs to the *actual* weight of God's reasons or the value of this state of affairs. But the defender of the Agapist Framework need not proceed with such inferences. Instead, defenders of this framework may proceed with inferences from a key aspect of God's character, namely love, conjoined with claims about value and divine action. The relevant value-claim is that things, characteristics, and actions are good insofar as (but not necessarily *because*) they resemble God, the most perfect being and plausible source of all goodness. The relevant claim about divine action is that God, being perfectly rational and motivated to do what He has good reasons for, has weighty reason to bring about beings, characteristics, and actions that resemble Himself (since these just are the foundational values) and thus is probably motivated to do so. On this second way of proceeding, the inferences are *conceptual*; they move from the nature of love, an understanding of ultimate values, and analysis of divine action to what God probably does. Hence, these inferences are very different from those that are challenged by the skeptical theist.

The following illustrations might help. If love is a defining divine characteristic, then God has weighty reasons to create a world that exemplifies this perfect love, and so might be expected to do so. Identifying with humans through condescending incarnation, redeeming them through self-sacrificial atonement, and glorifying them through intimate union with Himself are each profound expressions of love. These plausibly belong in the category of the best kinds of loving actions God could perform for humans. These are therefore the kinds of actions we would expect the perfectly loving God to do, in accordance with the Agapist Framework. Similarly, if God is fundamentally characterized by love, as indicated by the Agapist Framework, we should expect that the New Testament teaches that love *completes* the Christian ethic as a reflection of the divine character, as previously argued. Again, notice that these inferences are different from inferring that since we cannot discern a sufficiently good reason God might have for allowing the Holocaust (for example), God probably does not have one. So, the Agapist Framework arguably provides insight into who God is and what He does, while also allowing for skepticism regarding inferences from evil to the probable nonexistence of God or even the falsity of the Agapist Framework.

Moreover, the pairing of the Agapist Framework with skeptical theism does not preclude some of the theodicies previously listed. For example, if creatures who can love freely are among the most valuable kinds of creatures, since freedom and love are paramount features of God, then it is unsurprising that God would create humans with the relevant capacity. However, it is also plausible that this capacity is coupled with the ability to perform incredibly evil actions and makes divine hiddenness in some instances justified. Likewise, if providing creatures with the capacity "to make themselves" to resemble the character of God through a history of free choices sufficiently resembles God's aseity, God very well might grant humans this capacity. Yet this plausibly requires grappling with suffering and other obstacles. And so on.

But does this strategy not put arguments from evil back on the table with full force? For example, it might be argued that horrendous evils do not resemble God. Thus, God has weighty reason to prevent them, given the noted claims about value and divine action. Hence, horrendous evil counts against the articulated paradigm for divine action and so counts as strong evidence against the Agapist Framework. However, such reasoning invites the response that God, as just noted, has weighty reason on the Agapist Framework to grant humans freedom and obstacles to overcome, which may make possible horrendous evils. The point and counterpoint arguments may then continue, but they will need to proceed on conceptual grounds rather than on the kinds of inferences objected to by the skeptical theist (see Hendricks 2023a, 233–234).

Here, then, is a way of putting the pieces together with respect to the Agapist Framework and evil and divine hiddenness. The Agapist Framework presents a big-picture take on divine motivation. It predicts that God will act lovingly toward humans and perhaps creation more generally. It also predicts the possibility of certain kinds of evil and divine hiddenness, specifically, those which relate to free creatures who are tasked with character-building. However, there are other kinds of bad states of affairs that, from our perspective, are initially unexpected given the Agapist Framework. Yet we have reason to be skeptical of our ability to make all-things-considered judgments about what God would do or permit in some circumstances, unless they fall out of an analysis of God's character, especially love, together with noted claims about value and divine action.

The response developed in the preceding paragraphs gestures toward some of the ways that the Agapist Framework can account for the existence of the evil and hiddenness in the world (theodicies), and how the Agapist Framework can mitigate the evidential force of certain evils and instances of hiddenness (skeptical theism). A proponent of the Agapist Framework could maintain that these considerations ground a judgment that evil and hiddenness are just as well explained by the Agapist Framework as the other frameworks we have considered. Another way to judge these considerations is to acknowledge that evil and hiddenness might be better explained by another framework (e.g., the Holiness Framework), but in light of the strategies just mentioned, this comparative advantage is insignificant. And coupled with the other considerations given in favor of the Agapist Framework (both in terms of prior probability and explanatory power), we are justified in giving an all-things-considered judgment that the Agapist Framework is the most plausible framework considered in this Element.

7 Conclusion

The problem of divine motivation poses the challenge of providing a theoretical framework for understanding God's fundamental motives concerning creation, specifically humans. In this Element, four leading motivational frameworks of this kind have been discussed from a Christian perspective. We have argued that the Agapist Framework is the most plausible of the four.

Begin with a comparison between the Agapist Framework and Glorificationism. Recall, glorificationism entails the implausible conclusion that God cannot love creatures, or at least cannot love them richly. Relatedly, the framework also faces a kind of internal bind. Given that love is a key feature of God's intra-trinitarian life, one would expect God's expression of the most profound kinds of love and grace toward humans as among the best ways of glorifying Himself. But by making His own glory the primary aim of His human-directed acts, God is unable to manifest such expressions of love and grace. Of course, the glorificationist might retort that since all of God's actions *ad extra* are expressions of self-love, and God is maximally great, God in fact manifests the most profound expressions of love through, but not for, humans. However, this response arguably collides with the self-giving love found in Christ, who gave himself for humans. Each of these problems is eluded by the Agapist Framework.

In comparison to the Holiness Framework, the Agapist Framework has the advantage in theological predictive power. Among other things, the latter framework better predicts (i) the existence of creation, (ii) divine covenants as attested by Scripture, (iii) God's intimate indwelling in creation, and (iv) the content of Scripture's salvation arc, specifically as found in the person and work of Christ. A primary apparent advantage of the Holiness Framework concerns its mitigation of the problems of evil and divine hiddenness. We recognize that for many this is an enormous benefit of the Holiness Framework and the Achilles' heel of the Agapist Framework. However, the Holiness Framework arguably does not predict certain theodicies as well as the Agapist Framework. That, coupled with the other resources discussed for dealing with these problems on the Agapist Framework, arguably indicates that the Holiness Framework does not fare as well as the Agapist Framework, all things considered.

The comparison between the Agapist Framework and Morality Framework is more complicated. Plausibly, the Agapist Framework just is a version of the Morality Framework, perhaps a kind of virtue theory wherein the most significant virtue is love. If this is right, then it may look as if the Morality Framework is more probable than the Agapist Framework for the simple reason that general theories are often more likely than more specific theories, given the additional (and potentially false) commitments of the latter. One response would be to concede the point but argue that the Agapist Framework is the best version of the Morality Framework, and so worth adopting.

But consider this response on behalf of the Agapist Framework. While the Morality Framework is more intrinsically probable (due to it being less specific), it is unclear that its total prior probability is higher than the Agapist Framework. The arguments used to bolster the prior probability of the Morality Framework (i.e., perfect being theology, worship-worthiness, God as the ground of moral goodness, and the epistemic advantage over the evil-god challenge) plausibly work just as well to bolster the prior probability of the Agapist Framework. The Agapist Framework also enjoys additional prior probabilistic support from the doctrine of the Trinity, wherein love is central to the divine life.

Moreover, the Agapist Framework appears to possess greater explanatory power than the bare Morality Framework. This is because the assessment of the explanatory power of a given framework requires it to be sufficiently content-rich. To say merely that God is good does not tell us much about what to expect of Him. By contrast, the Agapist Framework is sufficiently precise. So, as argued, it has great theological predictive power, plausibly much greater than the mere claim that God is fundamentally motivated by moral norms.

Take, for example, the Word's incarnation and self-giving atonement to redeem and glorify humans. Are these the sort of actions that are predicted by the Morality Framework? That depends upon the details. If one thinks that God is fundamentally motivated by justice/righteousness or duty, the answer appears to be "no." Yet such divine actions, we have argued, are not so surprising on the Agapist Framework. The point is that it is reasonable to conclude that the generic form of the Morality Framework is not as overall probable as the Agapist Framework due to the latter's superior explanatory power and comparable, if not greater, prior probability.

However, none of this is meant to be the last word on the problem of divine motivation. Our treatment of the relevant issues has needed to be brief, partial, and at times contentious and assumptive. Nonetheless, we hope we have advanced the discussion on a comparative assessment of divine motivational frameworks and upheld the Agapist Framework as a reasonable view worthy of further consideration and defense.

References

Adams, Robert Merrihew (1972). "Must God Create the Best?" *Philosophical Review* 81 (3): 317–332.

Adams, Robert Merrihew (1999). *Finite and Infinite Goods: A Framework for Ethics*. Oxford: Oxford University Press.

Alston, William P. (1990). "Some Suggestions for Divine Command Theorists." In Michael Beaty, ed., *Christian Theism and the Problems of Philosophy*. South Bend, IN: University of Notre Dame Press, 303–326.

Anderson, Elizabeth (1995). *Value in Ethics and Economics*. Cambridge, MA: Harvard University Press.

Anglin, Bill and Stewart Goetz (1982). "Evil Is Privation." *International Journal for Philosophy of Religion* 13 (1): 3–12.

Athanasius of Alexandria (1954). "On the Incarnation." In Edward R. Hardy, ed., *Christology of the Later Fathers*, Archibald Robertson, trans. Louisville, KY: Westminster John Knox Press, 55–110.

Baggett, David and Jerry Walls (2011). *Good God: The Theistic Foundations of Morality*. Oxford: Oxford University Press.

Ballard, Brian Scott (2024). "The Threat of Anti-Theism: What Is at Stake in the Axiology of God?" *The Philosophical Quarterly* 74 (2): 408–430.

Bavinck, Herman (2004). *Reformed Dogmatics, Volume 2: God and Creation*, John Bolt, ed., John Vriend, trans. Grand Rapids, MI: Baker Academic.

Beale, Gregory Kimball (2014). *The Temple and the Church's Mission: A Biblical Theology of the Dwelling Place of God*. Downers Grove, IL: IVP Academic.

Bergmann, Michael (2009). "Skeptical Theism and the Problem of Evil." In Michael C. Rea and Thomas P. Flint, eds., *Oxford Handbook of Philosophical Theology*. Oxford: Oxford University Press, 374–402.

Berkhof, Louis (2017). *Systematic Theology*, Anthony Uyl ed. Woodstock, ON: Devoted Publishing.

Borg. Marcus J. (1998). *Conflict, Holiness, and Politics in the Teachings of Jesus*. Harrisburg, PA: Trinity Press International.

Boyd, Gregory A. (2001). *Satan and the Problem of Evil*. Downers Grove, IL: IVP Academic.

Boyd, Gregory A. (2017). *The Crucifixion of the Warrior God: Interpreting the Old Testament's Violent Portraits of God in Light of the Cross*. Minneapolis, MN: Fortress Press.

Brümmer, Vincent (1993). *The Model of Love: A Study in Philosophical Theology*. Cambridge: Cambridge University Press.

References

Calvin, John (1960). *Institutes of the Christian Religion*, John T. McNeill, ed., Ford Lewis Battles, trans. Louisville, KY: Westminster John Knox Press.

Chang, Ruth (2002). "The Possibility of Parity." *Ethics*, 112: 659–688.

Charnock, Stephen (1979). *The Existence and Attributes of God*, Vol. 2. Grand Rapids, MI: Baker Books.

Clayton, Philip (1997). *God and Contemporary Science*. Grand Rapids, MI: Eerdmans.

Climenhaga, Nevin (Forthcoming). "If We Can't Tell What Theism Predicts, We Can't Tell Whether God Exists: Skeptical Theism and Bayesian Arguments from Evil." *Oxford Studies in Philosophy of Religion*, Vol. 11.

Collins, Robin (2013). "The Connection-Building Theodicy." In Justin P. McBrayer and Daniel Howard-Snyder, eds., *The Blackwell Companion to the Problem of Evil*. Oxford: Wiley, 222–235.

Conee, Earl (1994). "The Nature and the Impossibility of Moral Perfection." *Philosophy and Phenomenological Research* 54 (4): 815–825.

Couenhoven, Jesse (2016). "The Problem of God's Immutable Freedom." In Kevin Timpe and Daniel Speak, eds., *Free Will and Theism: Connections, Contingencies, and Concerns*. Oxford: Oxford University Press, 277–293.

Craig, William Lane (2023). "Is God's Moral Perfection Reducible to His Love?" *Religions* 14: 1–9.

Crisp, Oliver D. (Forthcoming). *Metatheology: Foundational Issues in Divinity*.

Crisp, Oliver D. (2012). *Jonathan Edwards on God and Creation*. Oxford: Oxford University Press.

Crisp, Oliver D. (2021). "The Importance of Model Building in Theology." In James M. Arcadi and James T. Turner, Jr., eds., *T&T Clark Handbook of Analytic Theology*. London: T&T Clark, 9–19.

Cullison, Andrew (2010). "Two Solutions to the Problem of Divine Hiddenness." *American Philosophical Quarterly* 47 (2): 119–134.

Cuneo, Terence and Jada Twedt Strabbing (2023). "Wholly Good, Holy God." *Journal of Analytic Theology* 11 (1): 411–423.

Davies, Brian (2006). *The Reality of God and the Problem of Evil*. London: Continuum.

Davies, Brian (2011). *Thomas Aquinas on God and Evil*. Oxford: Oxford University Press.

Dodds, Michael J. (1986). *The Unchanging God of Love: A Study of the Teaching of St. Thomas Aquinas on Divine Immutability in View of Certain Contemporary Criticism of This Doctrine*. Fribourg: Éditions Universitaires.

Draper, Paul (2019). "What If God Makes Hard Choices?" In Lara Buchak, Dean W. Zimmerman, and Philip Swenson, eds., *Oxford Studies in the Philosophy of Religion*, Vol. 9. Oxford: Oxford University Press, 18–30.

Echavarría, Agustín (2022). "Can a Metaphysically Perfect God Have Moral Virtues and Duties? Re-Reading Aquinas." *American Catholic Philosophical Quarterly* 96 (3): 381–402.

Edwards, Jonathan (1957). *Freedom of the Will*, Vol. 1 of *The Works of Jonathan Edwards*, Paul Ramsey, ed., New Haven, CT: Yale University Press.

Edwards, Jonathan (1989). *Ethical Writings*, Vol. 8 of *The Works of Jonathan Edwards*, Paul Ramsey, ed. New Haven, CT: Yale University Press.

Edwards, Jonathan (1997). "The Terrors of Hell Are Exceeding Great." In Harry Stout, ed., *Sermons and Discourses 1723–1729*, *The Works of Jonathan Edwards*, Vol. 14. New Haven, CT: Yale University Press, 302–329.

Edwards, Jonathan (2001). "The Justice of God in the Damnation of Sinners." In M. X. Lesser, ed., *Sermons and Discourses, 1734–1738*, *The Works of Jonathan Edwards*, Vol. 19. New Haven, CT: Yale University Press, 340–377.

Ekstrom, Laura W. (2021). *God, Suffering, and the Value of Free Will*. Oxford: Oxford University Press.

Elmore, Benjamin (2024). "What If a Teleological Conception of Value Is False?" *Sophia*: 1–8.

Evans, C. Stephen (2013). *God and Moral Obligation*. Oxford: Oxford University Press.

Fleischacker, Samuel (2023). "God's Things: An Essay in Secondary Holiness." *Journal of Analytic Theology* 11 (1): 421–436.

Frankfurt, Harry G. (2009). *The Reasons of Love*. Princeton, NJ: Princeton University Press.

Garcia, Laura L. (2009). "Moral Perfection." In Thomas P. Flint and Michael C. Rea, eds., *The Oxford Handbook of Philosophical Theology*. Oxford: Oxford University Press, 217–238.

Göcke, Benedikt and Christian Tapp, eds. (2019). *The Infinity of God: New Perspectives in Theology and Philosophy*. Notre Dame, IN. University of Notre Dame.

Green, Christopher R. (2016). "A Compatibicalvinist Demonstrative-Goods Defense." In David E. Alexander and Daniel M. Johnson, eds., *Calvinism and the Problem of Evil*. Eugene, OR: Pickwick, 233–247.

Gregory of Nyssa (1978). *The Life of Moses*. Abraham J. Malherbe and Everett Ferguson, trans. Mahwah, NJ: Paulist Press.

Griffin, James (1986). *Well-Being: Its Meaning, Measurement and Importance*. Oxford: Clarendon Press.

Hadsell, Nick (Unpublished). "Our Divine Father's Response to Our Suffering."

Hanson, Anthony Tyrrell (1957). *Wrath of the Lamb*. London: S.P.C.K.

References

Hart, Matthew J. (2016). "Calvinism and the Problem of Evil." In David E. Alexander and Daniel M. Johnson, eds., *Calvinism and the Problem of Evil*. Eugene, OR: Pickwick, 248–272.

Hasker, William (2010). "All Too Skeptical Theism." *International Journal for Philosophy of Religion* 68: 15–29.

Hendricks, Perry (2023a). *Skeptical Theism*. New York: Palgrave Macmillan.

Hendricks, Perry (2023b). "The Proper Basicality of Belief in God and the Evil-God Challenge." *Religious Studies* 59: 55–62.

Hichem, Naar (2022). *The Rationality of Love*. New York: Oxford University Press.

Hill, Daniel (2005). *Divinity and Maximal Greatness*. London: Routledge.

Hill, William J. (1984). "Does Divine Love Entail Suffering in God?" In Bowman L. Clarke and Eugene Thomas Long, eds., *God and Temporality*. New York: New Era Books, 55–72.

Hoffman, Joshua and Gary S. Rosenkrantz (2002). *The Divine Attributes*. Malden, MA: Blackwell.

Howard-Snyder, Daniel (1996). "The Argument from Divine Hiddenness." *Canadian Journal of Philosophy* 26 (3): 433–453.

Howard-Snyder, Frances (2005). "On These Two Commandments Hang All the Law and the Prophets." *Faith and Philosophy* 22 (1): 3–20.

Howard-Snyder, Frances (2017). "Divine Freedom." *Topoi* 36 (4): 651–656.

Jordan, Jeffrey (2012). "The Topography of Divine Love." *Faith and Philosophy* 29 (1): 53–69.

Jordan, Jeff (2015). "The Topography of Divine Love." *Faith and Philosophy* 32 (2): 182–187.

Jordan, Jeff (2020). "The Limits of Divine Love." In James M. Arcadi, Oliver D. Crisp, and Jordan Wessling, eds., *Love, Divine and Human: Contemporary Essays in Systematic and Philosophical Theology*. London: T&T Clark, 81–95.

Kemp, Dan (2022). "Created Goodness and the Goodness of God: Divine Ideas and the Possibility of Creaturely Value." *Religious Studies* 58 (3): 534–546.

Kretzmann, Norman (1991). "A General Problem of Creation: Why Would God Create Anything at All?" In Scott MacDonald, ed., *Being and Goodness*. Ithaca, NY: Cornell University Press, 208–228.

Kvanvig, Jonathan L. (1993). *The Problem of Hell*. Oxford. Oxford University Press.

Kvanvig, Jonathan L. (2021). *Depicting Deity: A Metatheological Approach*. Oxford: Oxford University Press.

Layman, C. Stephen (2022). *God: Eight Enduring Questions*. Notre Dame, IN: University of Notre Dame Press.

Lebens, Samuel (2024). "The Apple of God's Eye: A Biblical Account of Holiness." *Religious Studies*. Published online: 1–15.
Leftow, Brian (1989). "Necessary Moral Perfection." *Pacific Philosophical Quarterly* 70 (2): 240–260.
Leftow, Brian (2006). "Divine Simplicity." *Faith and Philosophy* 23 (4): 365–380.
Leftow, Brian (2013). "God's Deontic Perfection." *Res Philosophica*, 90: 69–95.
Leftow, Brian (2017). "Two Pictures of Divine Choice." In Hugh J. McCann, ed., *Free Will and Classical Theism: The Significance of Freedom in Perfect Being Theology*. New York: Oxford University Press, 152–172.
Leftow, Brian (2019). "Infinite Goodness." In Benedikt Paul Göcke and Christian Tapp, eds., *The Infinity of God: New Perspectives in Theology and Philosophy*. Notre Dame, IN. University of Notre Dame, 296–316.
Lewis, Charles (1983). "Divine Goodness and Worship Worthiness." *International Journal for Philosophy of Religion* 14 (2): 143–158. http://dx.doi.org/10.1007/BF00136891.
Loke, Andrew Ter Ern (2023). "A New Moral Argument for the Existence of God." *International Journal for Philosophy of Religion* 93 (1): 25–38.
Luke, Sean (2024). "Against Divine Amorism: An Argument for Glorificationism." *Journal of Analytic Theology* 12 (1): 17–28.
Manis, R. Zachary (2016). "'Eternity Will Nail Him to Himself': The Logic of Damnation in Kierkegaard's *The Sickness unto Death*." *Religious Studies* 52 (3): 287–314.
Mariña, Jacqueline (2021). "Review of Mark Murphy *Divine Holiness and Divine Action*." *European Journal for Philosophy of Religion* 13 (4): 193–197.
McCall, Thomas H. (2008). "We Believe in God's Sovereign Goodness: A Rejoinder to John Piper." *Trinity Journal* 29: 235–246.
McClymond, Michael J. (1995). "Sinners in the Hands of a Virtuous God: Ethics and Divinity in Jonathan Edwards's *End of Creation*." *Zeitschrift Für Neuere Theologiegeschicte* 2 (1): 1–22.
McClymond, Michael J. and Gerald R. McDermott (2011). *The Theology of Jonathan Edwards*. New York: Oxford University Press.
McFarland, Ian A. (2014). *From Nothing: A Theology of Creation*. Louisville, KY: Westminster John Knox Press.
Menssen, Sandra and Thomas D. Sullivan (2007). *The Agnostic Inquirer: Revelation from a Philosophical Standpoint*. Grand Rapids, MI: Eerdmans.
Middleton, J. Richard (2014). *A New Heaven and a New Earth: Reclaiming Biblical Eschatology*. Grand Rapids, MI: Baker Academic.

Morris, Thomas V. (1987). *Anselmian Explorations*. Notre Dame, IN: University of Notre Dame Press.

Morriston, Wes (2000). "What's So Good about Moral Freedom?" *Philosophical Quarterly* 50 (200): 344–358.

Moser, Paul K. (2008). *The Elusive God: Reorienting Religious Epistemology*. Cambridge: Cambridge University Press.

Murphy, Mark C. (2017). *God's Own Ethics: Norms of Divine Agency and the Argument from Evil*. Oxford: Oxford University Press.

Murphy, Mark (2019). "Perfect Goodness." *Stanford Encyclopedia of Philosophy* (Winter 2021 Ed.), Edward N. Zalta (ed.), https://plato.stanford.edu/archives/win2021/entries/perfect-goodness/.

Murphy, Mark C. (2021). *Divine Holiness and Divine Action*. Oxford: Oxford University Press.

Murphy, Mark C. (2023). "The Difference Holiness Makes." *Journal of Analytic Theology* 11 (1): 470–488.

Murray, Michael J. (2002). "Deus Absconditus." In Daniel Howard-Snyder and Paul K. Moser, eds., *Divine Hiddenness: New Essays*. New York: Cambridge University Press, 62–82.

Murray, Michael and Michael Rea (2008). *An Introduction to the Philosophy of Religion*. Cambridge: Cambridge University Press.

Nagasawa, Yujin (2017). *Maximal God: A New Defense of Perfect Being Theism*. Oxford: Oxford University Press.

Nygren, Anders (1982). *Agape and Eros: The Christian Idea of Love*. Philip S. Watson, trans. Chicago, IL: University of Chicago Press.

Oddie, Graham (2005). *Value, Reality, and Desire*. Oxford: Oxford University Press.

Oord, Thomas Jay (2010). *Defining Love: A Philosophical, Scientific, and Theological Engagement*. Grand Rapids, MI: Brazos Press.

Oord, Thomas Jay (2015). *The Uncontrolling Love of God*. Downers Grove, IL: IVP Academic.

Oppy, Graham (2014). *Describing Gods: An Investigation of Divine Attributes*. Cambridge: Cambridge University Press.

Otto, Rudolph (1923). *The Idea of the Holy*. John W. Harvey, trans. Oxford: Oxford University Press.

Pannenberg, Wolfhart (1991). *Systematic Theology*, Vol. 1. Geoffrey W. Bromiley, trans. Grand Rapids, MI: Eerdmans.

Parker, Ross (2013). "Deep and Wide: A Response to Jeff Jordan on Divine Love." *Faith and Philosophy* 30 (4): 444–461.

References

Pereboom, Derk (2005). "Free Will, Evil, and Divine Providence." In Andrew Chignell and Andrew Dole, eds., *God and the Ethics of Belief.* Cambridge: Cambridge University Press, 77–98.

Peterson, Michael, William Hasker, Bruce Reichenbach, and David Basinger (2013). *Reason and Religious Belief: An Introduction to the Philosophy of Religion.* 5th ed. Oxford: Oxford University Press.

Poston, Ted (2020). "The Intrinsic Probability of Grand Explanatory Theories." *Faith and Philosophy* 37 (4): 401–420.

Pruss, Alexander R. (2012). *One Body: An Essay in Christian Sexual Ethics.* Notre Dame, IN: University of Notre Dame Press.

Quinn, Philip (1992). "God, Moral Perfection, and Possible Worlds." In Michael Peterson, ed., *The Problem of Evil: Selected Readings.* Notre Dame, IN. University of Notre Dame Press, 428–443.

Rauser, Randal (2021). *Jesus Loves the Canaanites: Biblical Genocide in the Light of Moral Intuition.* Canada: 2 Cup Press.

Raz, Joseph (1999). *Practical Reason and Norms.* Oxford: Oxford University Press.

Rea, Michael C. (2018). *The Hiddenness of God.* Oxford: Oxford University Press.

Rea, Michael C. (2022) "Love for God and Self-Annihilation." *Faith and Philosophy* 39 (4): 511–534.

Rigney, Joe (2023). *Communicating God's Trinitarian Fullness: An Exposition of Jonathan Edwards' End for Which God Created the Word.* Landrum, SC: Davenant Press.

Rogers, Katherin (2000). *Perfect Being Theology.* Edinburgh: Edinburgh University Press.

Rowe, William L. (2003). *Can God Be Free?* Oxford: Clarendon Press.

Rubio, Daniel (Forthcoming). "Intrinsically Good, God Created Them." *Oxford Studies in Philosophy of Religion.* Oxford: Oxford University Press.

Rutledge, Jonathan C. and Jordan Wessling (2023). "God of Holy Love: Toward an Agapist Alternative to Mark Murphy's Holiness Framework for Divine Action." *Journal of Analytic Theology* 11 (1): 437–456.

Satta, Mark (2020). "Is There a Duty-Generating Special Relationship of Creator to Creature?" *Sophia* 59, 637–649.

Scanlon, Thomas Michael (1998). *What We Owe to Each Other.* Cambridge, MA: Harvard University Press.

Schellenberg, John L. (2015). *The Hiddenness Argument: Philosophy's New Challenge to Belief in God.* Oxford: Oxford University Press.

Schultz, Walter J. (2014a). "Jonathan Edwards' Argument That God's End in Creation Must Manifest His Supreme Self-regard." *Jonathan Edwards Studies* 4 (1), 81–103.

Schultz, Walter J. (2014b). "Jonathan Edwards' Philosophical Argument for God's End in Creation." *Jonathan Edwards Studies* 4 (3), 297–326.

Schultz, Walter J. (2020). *Jonathan Edwards' Concerning the End for Which God Created the World: Exposition, Analysis, and Philosophical Implications.* Göttingen: Vandenhoeck & Ruprecht.

Seibert, Eric A. (2016). "Recent Research on Divine Violence in the Old Testament (with Special Attention to Christian Theological Perspectives)." *Currents in Biblical Research* 15 (1): 8–40.

Sijuwade, Joshua (2024). "The Love Argument for the Trinity: A Reformulation." *TheoLogica, an International Journal for Philosophy of Religion and Philosophical Theology*, 9 (1): 1–35. https://doi.org/10.14428/thl.v9i1.80503.

Stump, Eleonore (1992). "God's Obligations." *Philosophical Perspectives* 6: 475–491.

Stump, Eleonore (2010). *Wandering in Darkness: Narrative and the Problem of Suffering.* Oxford: Oxford University Press.

Swinburne, Richard (1994). *The Christian God.* Oxford: Clarendon Press.

Swinburne, Richard (1998). *Providence and the Problem of Evil.* Oxford: Clarendon Press.

Swinburne, Richard (2003). *The Resurrection of God Incarnate.* Oxford: Clarendon Press.

Swinburne, Richard (2004). *The Existence of God.* 2nd Ed. Oxford: Clarendon Press.

Swinburne, Richard (2016). *The Coherence of Theism.* 2nd Ed. Oxford: Clarendon Press.

Symes, Jack (2024). *Defeating the Evil-God Challenge.* London: Bloomsbury Academic.

Talbott, Thomas (2020). "In Defense of the Loving Parent Analogy." In Oliver D. Crisp, James M. Arcadi, and Jordan Wessling, eds., *Love, Divine and Human: Contemporary Essays in Systematic Theology.* London: T&T Clark, 97–112

Taylor, Gabriele (1975–1976). "Love." *Proceedings of the Aristotelian Society* 76: 147–164.

Timpe, Kevin (2016a). "The Best Thing in Life Is Free: The Compatibility of Divine Freedom and God's Essential Moral Perfection." In Hugh J. McCann, ed., *Free Will and Classical Theism: The Significance of Freedom in Perfect Being Theology.* Oxford: Oxford University Press, 133–151.

Timpe, Kevin (2016b). "God's Freedom, God's Character." In Kevin Timpe and Daniel Speak, eds., *Free Will and Theism: Connections, Contingencies, and Concerns.* Oxford: Oxford University Press, 277–293.

Torrance, Thomas F. (1996). *The Christian Doctrine of God, One Being Three Persons.* Edinburgh: T&T Clark.

References

Tucker, Chris (2020). "Divine Satisficing and the Ethics of the Problem of Evil." *Faith and Philosophy* 37 (1): 32–56.

van Driel, Edwin Chr. (2008). *Incarnation Anyway: Arguments for Supralapsarian Christology.* Oxford: Oxford University Press.

Vicens, Leigh (Forthcoming). "Divine Holiness and the Axiology of Theism." *Faith and Philosophy.*

Weinandy, Thomas (2000). *Does God Suffer?* Notre Dame, IN: University of Notre Dame Press.

Wessling, Jordan (2020a). *Love Divine: A Systematic Account of God's Love for Humanity.* Oxford: Oxford University Press.

Wessling, Jordan (2020b). "A Love that Speaks in Harsh Tones: On the Superiority of Divine Communicative Punishment." In James Arcadi, Oliver Crisp, and Jordan Wessling, eds., *Love, Divine and Human: Contemporary Essays in Systematic and Philosophical Theology.* London: T&T Clark, 145–164.

Wessling, Jordan (2021). "Divine Goodness and Love." In James M. Arcadi and James T. Turner, eds., *T&T Clark Companion to Analytic Theology.* London: T&T Clark, 141–154.

Wessling, Jordan (2022). "Responses to Love Divine's Respondents." *Philosophia Christi* 24 (1): 47–62.

Wessling, Jordan (2023). "The Toughest of Loves." *Journal of Analytic Theology* 11: 110–131.

Wielenberg, Erik J. (2017). "Intrinsic Value and Love: Three Challenges for *God's Own Ethics*," *Religious Studies* 53: 551–557.

Williams, Daniel K. (2021). "When the Canaanite Conquest Met the Enlightenment: How Christian Apologists of the English Enlightenment Harmonized the Biblical Canaanite Conquest with the Moral Values of the Eighteenth Century." *Church History* 90 (3): 579–602.

Wilson, Luke (2022). "Perfect Freedom and God's Hard Choices." *Faith and Philosophy* 39 (2): 291–312.

Wilson, Luke (2024). "Murphy's Anselmian Theism and the Problem of Evil." *Religious Studies* 60 (4): 549–563.

Wood, William (2016). "Modeling Mystery." *Scientia et Fides* 4 (1): 39–59.

Wynn, Mark. (2022). "Some Reflections on Richard's Swinburne's 'God's Moral Goodness'." *Philosophy of Religion: Analytic Researches* 22 (6): 56–66.

Yadav, Sameer (2023). "All Shall Love Me and Despair! Murphy on Divine Holiness." *Journal of Analytic Theology* 11 (1): 458–469.

Zagzebski, Linda (2004). *Divine Motivation Theory.* Cambridge: Cambridge University Press.

Acknowledgments

We are grateful for the support we received in the production of this Element. Our gratitude goes to Aaron Brown, Mark Hamilton, and Ryan West for providing comments on earlier drafts of one or more of this Element's sections. Special thanks also to Logan Gage and Steven Nemes for graciously commenting upon the entire Element. The following individuals also discussed ideas or provided resources that were integral to the completion of this manuscript: Brian Ballard, Nick Hadsell, Layne Hancock, Perry Hendricks, Sean Luke, Leigh Vicens, Luke Wilson, and Chris Woznicki. These people helped to improve this Element greatly (whatever its remaining shortcomings). We are also indebted to Mark Murphy for his trailblazing work on divine deliberative frameworks from which we have benefited greatly. Finally, we appreciate Michael Peterson in his capacity as editor of The Problems of God series for guiding this Element to publication.

Jordan Wessling wishes to dedicate this Element to Oliver D. Crisp, for his friendship and mentorship over the years, including many discussions about the motives and purposes of God. Ross Parker dedicates this Element to his wife Rachel, for her support during this writing project, and for her deep and abiding love.

Cambridge Elements⁼

The Problems of God

Series Editor
Michael L. Peterson
Asbury Theological Seminary
Michael L. Peterson is Professor of Philosophy at Asbury Theological Seminary. He is the author of *God and Evil* (Routledge); *Monotheism, Suffering, and Evil* (Cambridge University Press); *With All Your Mind* (University of Notre Dame Press); *C. S. Lewis and the Christian Worldview* (Oxford University Press); *Evil and the Christian God* (Baker Book House); and *Philosophy of Education: Issues and Options* (Intervarsity Press). He is co-author of *Reason and Religious Belief* (Oxford University Press); *Science, Evolution, and Religion: A Debate about Atheism and Theism* (Oxford University Press); and *Biology, Religion, and Philosophy* (Cambridge University Press). He is editor of *The Problem of Evil: Selected Readings* (University of Notre Dame Press). He is co-editor of *Philosophy of Religion: Selected Readings* (Oxford University Press) and *Contemporary Debates in Philosophy of Religion* (Wiley-Blackwell). He served as General Editor of the Blackwell monograph series Exploring Philosophy of Religion and is founding Managing Editor of the journal *Faith and Philosophy*.

About the Series
This series explores problems related to God, such as the human quest for God or gods, contemplation of God, and critique and rejection of God. Concise, authoritative volumes in this series will reflect the methods of a variety of disciplines, including philosophy of religion, theology, religious studies, and sociology.

Cambridge Elements⁼

The Problems of God

Elements in the Series

C.S. Lewis and the Problem of God
David Werther

God and Happiness
Matthew Shea

God and the Problem of Epistemic Defeaters
Joshua Thurow

The Problem of God in Jewish Thought
Jerome Gellman With Joseph (Yossi) Turner

The Trinity
Scott M. Williams

The Problem of Divine Personality
Andrew M. Bailey and Bradley Rettler

Religious Trauma
Michelle Panchuk

Embodiment, Dependence, and God
Kevin Timpe

The Problem of God in Thomas Reid
James Foster

The Problem of God in Buddhism
Signe Cohen

God and Non-Human Animals
Simon Kittle

Divine Motivation and Humanity
Jordan Wessling and Ross Parker

A full series listing is available at: www.cambridge.org/EPOG

For EU product safety concerns, contact us at Calle de José Abascal, 56–1°, 28003 Madrid, Spain or eugpsr@cambridge.org.

www.ingramcontent.com/pod-product-compliance
Lightning Source LLC
LaVergne TN
LVHW020351260326
834688LV00045B/1657